Life
with a
CAPITAL
"L"

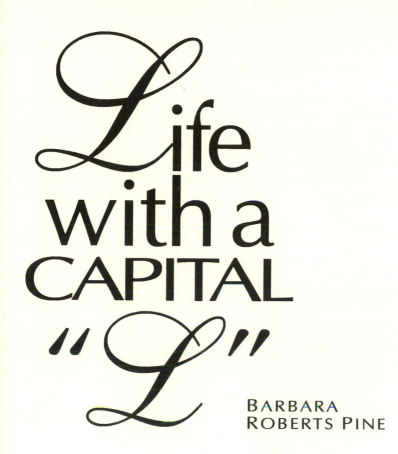

Life with a CAPITAL "L"

BARBARA
ROBERTS PINE

THOMAS NELSON
PUBLISHERS
Nashville

Published in Nashville, Tennessee, by Thomas Nelson, Inc., Publishers, and distributed in Canada by Word Communications, Ltd., Richmond, British Columbia.

The Bible version used in this publication is THE NEW KING JAMES VERSION. Copyright © 1979, 1980, 1982, Thomas Nelson, Inc., Publishers. Scripture quotations noted NRSV are from the New Revised Standard Version of the Bible. Copyright © 1989 by the Division of Christian Education of the National Council of the Churches of Christ in the United States of America. Scripture quotations noted KJV are from The King James Version of the Holy Bible.

Library of Congress Cataloging-in-Publication Data

Pine, Barbara Roberts, 1939–
    Life with a capital "L" / Barbara Roberts Pine.
      p.   cm.
    ISBN 0-8407-9205-0
    1. Christian life—1960– 2. Self-actualization—Religious aspects—Christianity. I. Title.
    BV4501.2.P5525   1994
    248.4—dc20   93–40824
                                          CIP

Printed in the United States of America.
1 2 3 4 5 6 — 98 97 96 95 94

CONTENTS

For Doug, Gordy, and Kimberly and for those they bring to our expanding family.

INTRODUCTION

Life—with a capital "L." That "L" can burden us with bundles heavier than a peasant's load. Occasionally it sweeps us up to unexpected delight by inviting us to lay aside tasks and obligations, to fly away. It was literally that sort of invitation I accepted last midwinter. I spent the turning of the New Year on a first-class flight from Los Angeles to Miami, Florida. The occasion was festive, circumstantially affordable, and spontaneous. How ready I was for the season's "peace on earth" or, in this case, in the air. I packed imagining a quiet, relaxed flight cradling me and my reading material in well-tended aloneness. I left every vestige of work at home.

My idealized version of travel lasted for about six minutes. It prevailed as I buckled myself into a large, leather seat and drank orange juice served before the captain's command to push off the gate. Then came reality, one that stretched through being stranded in Texas on my way home. But that is a different story. This one began by having unexpected company aboard the flight. A friend, a pilot, was "dead-heading" in order to work a trip originating in Miami.

Nick and I are members of the same church; he and my husband even work for the same company. Still, we had not visited in months. Big, friendly Nick had no visions of quiet, no illusions of reading for five hours; he was perfectly relaxed already, thank you, and upon seeing me seemingly unoccupied, he vacated his assigned seat, claimed the empty one next to me, and squared off for the vigorous sort of conversation our encounters always produce.

Simply put, our opinions are as contrary as coconuts and chili peppers. Our discussions are lively and discursive. We zip from A to Z, jump from hot topic to hot topic. We question each other on such subjects as gender roles and differences, advantages of being logical or emotional (I lean toward the former, he, the latter), the aurora borealis (I said discursive), or the practice of faith. Somewhere over Louisiana, I think, we volleyed between us the question of whether faith is more a matter of surrender or commitment.

Nick loves—yes, loves—the concept of surrender. Predictably, he loathes a favorite term of mine, the sniveling word *commitment*. Nick surrenders and God shapes his day. According to my friend, his job is to yield and watch the results. He earns my respect. Nick has whipped some tough obstacles. I suspect he even interprets his role in rupturing my tranquility as an outcome of surrender to God. But that is beside the point.

The point is that our discussion of commitment versus surrender pestered me long after this trip ended. I remembered as a child bending tabs of dresses and gowns over the shoulders and arms of paper dolls. Now, I found myself bending surrender and commitment over activities and attitudes of daily life, seeing how each fits, deciding which outfit I preferred. I preferred commitment. It is, after all, my sense of its fit (or rather, popular lack of it) in the ordinary run of human experience that motivates the writing of this book. Commitment? It is an act of giving in, a choice to surrender to something. "Aha!" shouts Nick in my mind. "See? You said 'surrender.' "

"Not so fast," my mind fires back. "There is a pivotal difference." My command of a situation is a snap when I mentally manage the discourse. Surrender means giving in, yes, but it lacks the element of *choosing* that commitment requires. Surrender requires passivity, and my observation is that, in the ordinary run of things, passivity seldom wears well.

Yes, it has its place. Surrender is a fitting response when choices are gone, like at the end of a war or a rifle barrel; in childhood, when a powerful sibling requests cooperation by hammerlock; for some, under the first crushing wave of crazy love; for others, when the love of God overwhelms. Passivity can be admirable. Unlike surrender, commitment is not co-erced. It is not quiet, it wiggles with energy. It is always active and free. It is an *act* of trusting, pledging, or consigning oneself to something. It reeks of risk and responsibility. It is a deciding word not a resigning word and that can alarm us. There is no question but that commitment-making plays an important role in real life and real life is what we are after.

If commitment is so important—and to me it is—I am puz-zled that we know so little about its occurrence. Surely, commitment presumes individual freedom and responsibility. "I just couldn't help it" nullifies human accountability in life circumstances; it eliminates the word *freedom* completely. Even diehard determinists find themselves rejecting this. The person who "chooses" to steal a stereo from a determinist darn well better prepare to face responsibility in a courtroom. The determinist's inconsistency will be there too. We may know little, but we know this: *freedom of choice attends commitment-making.*

Next, imagine finding the actual brain site of human volition. At that place, various influences battle for priority in decision-making: options, habits, memories, beliefs, and desires. Intellect and emotion square off there, yet neither owns our decisions outright. In *The Merchant of Venice,* Shakespeare tips his hat to emotion when he writes, "The brain may devise laws for the blood, but a hot temper leaps over a cold decree." Still, we must remember that while thought is emotionally colored, emotions are *thoughtfully* informed. Go figure.

With respect to complexity, the point is that *choices are influenced.* For instance, existing human character jumps into the fray and strongly influences commitment-making. But then, the argument is rightly made that the shape of one's character is molded by the pressure *of* commitments. What do we know for sure? Only that choices must occur or human will is paralyzed and that choices mean commitment to something. No wonder the admirable arts of philosophy, psychiatry, theology, and neurology all remain fairly coy when asked to explain the workings of choice. I only hope I have been vague enough!

Human character receives great attention in the pages of this book. Its influence may be complex, but its definition is not. Character is *that aggregate of behaviors and attitudes that distinguish each of us from all others.* Human distinctions are not dependent upon externals even though Advertising means to convince us otherwise. Labels on our clothing, the car we drive, a tag on our attache case, the beverage we drink create a distinctiveness by purchase.

In reality, behaviors and attitudes distinguish us. They affect everything we do, and affect everyone around us. Character and commitments describe a true self. Get real! Exactly. That is what I advocate. It is not always easy to do. It is not merely "surrendering" to an external idea.

When I use the term *real,* I mean authentic. I mean a person with mental and emotional energy (IQ is not the point), with a desire to experience and learn, one safely connected to other imperfect people and beneficially interested in them, aware but not jaded, a gatherer of nature's gifts not a hoarder of manufactured goods, sensitive to a moment or occasion, and moved by solid values. That is a fair start at definition.

I have an idea about real life, a simple one. But please imagine it written in a whisper. I feel safe saying it quietly because even though I am convinced of its incredible importance, it may sound outrageously dull.

In this book I advocate that we commit our character, our attitudes and behaviors, to nobility. Whoa! What? Nobility? In America? Where we have no aristocracy, where our heroes are entertainers and game players? Where violence is admired and excess encouraged? Where students and parents consider intelligent use of the brain an embarrassment? Where self-discipline is as rare as polio? Where employees regularly rip off businesses that frequently rip off both employees and the public? In this milieu we insert nobility? Exactly.

Granted, nobility is not only an unfamiliar modern practice, but the word itself sounds confining, hoity-toity, artificial, arrogant, extreme, yes? It is none of these and it has everything to do with being real. It is the opposite of common, the opposite of deceptive, it rejects ignorance, it values people, it seeks excellence, it is rare and honorable. It is a choice. It is a commitment to choice.

Personally, I think America could benefit from a liberal splattering of nobility. At least my observation is that individuals who commit to this quiet word experience life well. Not perfectly, not faultlessly, but well. I have never met, nor do I know any means for creating, a perfect or faultless person. People who actively risk habits of nobility are simply authentic. They commit to responsibility and they, uh, surrender passivity.

Being real in a frenetic, whirlwindy sort of life that technology imposes takes deliberateness. In an age of too many good (or evil) things to do, and too many good (or evil) ways to do them, in a social milieu encouraging contrived character and shallow relationships, in an age worn out by energy-saving devices, being real—in our settings, with others, with ourselves—requires deliberateness.

Without a commitment to something better, we are passively ruled by the convenient, the contiguous, the comfortable, the quick, the clever, the uncomplicated. Too frequently the reward of such things is cynicism, weariness, selfishness, a stunted spirit, and a defeated ego.

It's an "L" of a job, really. In fact, I think it will take at least seven capital *L*'s and a lifetime. The poet e. e. cummings understood this when he wrote,

> to be nobody but yourself in a world which is doing its best, night and day, to make you everybody else, means to fight the hardest battle which any human being can fight; and never stop fighting.

Lingering, Listening, Learning, Leaning, Loaning, Laughing, and Leaving are weapons of survival. We can learn to use them, one *L* at a time.

CHAPTER ONE

*L*ingering

I have lingered this morning. It is raining hard, the house is wonderfully quiet, and the coffee unusually good. I meant to finish unpacking from a trip completed yesterday, to get to my writing with haste. Instead, I have stayed in other situations longer than expected, and I have been reluctant to leave those distractions. By definition, I have lingered.

Usually, lingering happens unintentionally, as in staying to eat just a few more bites of German chocolate cake. Occasionally, we are wise enough to make it a deliberate and beneficial pause—as it was a few moments ago when I fell captive to the foggy, rain-pounded Puget Sound I love so. It cast its heavy, gray spell and ruled my attention like a worthy master rules a loyal pet. I turned from it refreshed and again set to work, searching through my old journals for a particular tidbit about my grandmother. It was meant to open this chapter. The tidbit eluded me, but reflection did not. I lingered over decades of penned pages, line upon line of past sorrows and joys, notes from my children, pasted bits of memorabilia, resolves, and accounts of experiences I thought then would never fade from memory but have. I paused at a page from 1981 where I wrote, "It's too bad emotions don't hemorrhage, then we would have to tend to their healing or die." The exact memory of what made that opinion so acute escapes me, but I am glad that in the midst of whatever it was, with a house full of teenagers and five or more schedules to juggle, I lingered long enough to record the thought.

On March 26, 1979, I wrote in the wee hours, obviously in a frivolous mood. I sketched a large female eye and beside it wrote,

Ode to Eyeliner

Oh, I remember well the day when black streaks
slipped easily round the way my eye shaped.
Staying where my fine brush led,
Heavy, smooth, it never bled
away from its planned channel.

I felt so proud . . . my flawless, wrinkle-free face allowed
such perfect application.

Eyeliner; black, dark brown, or beige;
in pencil, cake, or many ways,
was perfect eighteen years ago.

Oh, still I roll a wet brush on the cake,
Still a deft small line I make,
But if too much moisture gathers there,
color scatters everywhere
. . . through eighteen years of aging.

In 1979, in jest I confronted my waning youth. Pages away from that I found serious words on "grace" that came from watching a grasshopper feast on a peapod in our garden. I am fairly certain now that years ago when I lingered over sketches, ideas, and feelings, I wrested that time from better things "I should be doing." Should—ought—must—mustn't are powerful deterrents to lingering.

I still sometimes write in journals, but am much freer now to arrange the occasion than when my family and its demands were young. Then, lingering was exotic. I longed for it as surely as my children longed for birthdays. I worked and bartered for it, dearly paying powerful time-holders like motherhood, housewifery, community and church work, and the expectations of others.

I repacked journals and turned to the task of writing. That is, I meant to. The phone rang. It was our son, Gordy, who lives nearby. This was a good time for him to instruct me in the use of my computer's new modem. He wants to teach me to call him through it. Great. Fine. I tried to be excited. Gordy is light years ahead of me in the use of these machines, and I acknowledge a need to catch up some. How good, says the literature, to be able to "access" someone. How terribly more thrilling to "access" than simply to phone or call.

Now, with a mere jillion keystrokes, a stack of instructions, reading and typing, waiting and watching, I can do what seven finger-taps on a phone's dial, a few short rings, and my voice once did—reach my son. To say I lingered here is a bit of an understatement.

But, oh, how proud I am to report that after an hour or so of practice, I have the option to ignore my phone, turn on my computer, reach the right program, tap in the code, hear the horrible access tone, type a message, leave it in a "room" on Gordy's system, hope and pray he bothers to check his computer, to open the door of my message room there, read, and then access me . . . *if* my computer is on and my modem initializes correctly. Wow! The joys available to efficient people . . . but I should refrain from cynicism. In reality, lingering brought another slice of the modern world to me. I need that. I am quite apt to avoid modernity, here in my early middle age. Surely, runs my logic, I have learned enough, I have lingered enough over things, experiences, and people. I am inclined to justify a cessation of growth, but that inclination carries grave consequences.

Beneficial lingering, the capturing of our attention, staying at something good longer than expected, being reluctant to leave, is the *L* that applies a brake to runaway reluctance and fires momentum to flagging zeal. I have lingered this morning in nature's stormy mood, in memory's reflection, and in an exercise of growth. Now, I write to recommend this *L* as a necessity to being real. Lingering is a pause, whether joyous or painful, by which we are blessed. We must learn to linger for at least these three reasons: 1) to discover our world, 2) to discover others, 3) to discover ourselves. Am I surprised that God said that in order for us to know him, we must "be still." Linger.

Discovering Our Setting, Discovering Our World

Sometimes my journal is kept well, sometimes poorly. In it I frequently note my setting, like noticing the antics of a cocky blue jay I see outside now as I write. How well I describe him is less important than what the activity of description requires. It demands that I pause to pay attention, and paying attention is tricky.

My hunch is that most people remain keenly aware of the terrors and dangers in our world, but too rarely do we remember its abundant kindnesses. Harsh realities of experience can be pleasantly relieved by the antics of a river otter or by a cat stalking a grasshopper. Only, we must deliberately watch for such things. We must be willing to be beneficially distracted. A spider's web, jeweled by dew, is always beautiful whether it is found in an exotic jungle or a cluttered alley. Only, we have to pause and pay attention if we hope to receive the gift.

We moderns live in our world like the kid who frantically digs through a Christmas stocking, grabbing the contents, working hard to get to the end. And when he gets there? The experience is over, as our lives will be. Did he see the stocking? Was it made especially for him by someone who loves him? Did he notice? What do we see, hear, touch, savor, smell, or learn from that which holds our life? Will we miss the texture and shape of our world? Whether we carelessly neglect setting depends on whether we have learned to value the "place" provided us for getting to the end of things, of experiences, of relationships, of life.

Lingering to discover setting does not require an ideal place. Numerous people, including Corrie Ten Boom and Victor Frankl, learned beneficial lingering in concentration camps. Disease, too, can be a setting for great sculpting of character. Loss dares us to linger and learn. Setting *is*. Just is. It can be fierce or fine. All situations allow for careless attitudes, any can lend to being real.

My friend Linda died last year. She hoped to reach her fiftieth birthday but did not. As she lived, in the midst of busyness and not waiting for ideal moments, Linda embraced her world.

Years ago we painted the front of my house while our combined six children ran circles around us, squealing, laughing, crying, fighting, and making demands. In the midst of our task and the distractions, Linda noticed an abandoned bird's nest. She promptly set brushes and efficiency aside, brought the nest down, sat on a porch step and touched it, turned it, tested its strength, examined its structural wonders, mused aloud about its possible history, and exhibited to our six children the value of lingering over natural things, of feeling the wonderful impatience required in waiting for spring and eggs and baby birds. She shared the reality of worrying about predators and wind and all the things that are able to threaten our treasures and our dearest hopes. But treasures and dear hopes do not die because they can be threatened. Ah, how real she was.

Linda's flower beds held an arrangement of smooth rocks which she gathered in bulging pockets ("just one more") during our walks on the beaches near my house, or from the Colorado mountains which she loved and near which she lived. Those rocks were heavy with setting and worthy of being toted in suitcases between states in order to be enjoyed, briefly lingered over after work or between the many obligations that filled her days.

Now, *my* less-than-perfect flower beds hold Shasta daisies, some Brown-eyed Susans, and a rock or two from the beach. From a hospital bed Linda followed in her mind the progress of daisies in her yard, the ones growing around the rocks from California beaches. She knew they would bloom on the Fourth of July and they did. We took some to her.

A few days later when she died, I spent the day in my yard digging in earth she loved so fervently, arranging rocks and planting daisies to remind me, next spring, of our years of friendship, and as a way of lingering in memory before I knew how to linger in grief. Finding gifts of goodness in our setting brings nobility to our lives. Only, we must pause.

A small white feather in one of my journals reminds me of a mean-spirited parakeet, Caspian, that for years ruled my desk and chewed on my books. Stroking the feather brings delight. I loved the way that arrogant creature pulled me away from thought and suggested that the world was not all inside my head. I cannot live without noticing natural things, without sensing my setting. It quiets my pace and distracts my sorrow, it heightens my joy, and moderates my extremes. It reminds me of how much I do not know, how much mystery remains in being human.

I still do occasionally stretch out under a blossoming orange tree or under the massive pine in the corner of our yard. Especially if I feel sorry for myself. When my eyes are closed and I smell the fragrances, I fret less readily over a harsh exchange, rooms that need painting, or the possibility of a manuscript being rejected. I may weep stretched out under a tree, but there I do so differently than when lying on my bed or closed privately in a room. There are relationships I cannot seem to fix, the deaths of people I love, and a passel of dashed dreams. I cannot avoid the impact of such real things.

Thank goodness for clouds that resemble Aunt Edna's scowl, for the tide, a star, the boggling and wonderfully distractive task of figuring the path of the moon, a breeze in a bush, the journey of a pillbug across a porch, the wait and the weight involved in a drop of water about to fall, the way a horse or cow can shimmy their skin and we cannot, warm dirt under bare feet, mud, the safe and silly company of dogs. For hot tea or coffee in a special mug, for letters, books, and favorite tables in a special restaurant. Authentic life in a highly artificial world calls for the discovery of setting.

Lingering in Order to Discover Others

A World of Information

To function well in our crowded world we need to know things about people. But we have little time, thank you, for discovery questions. So what a relief to learn that lingering is unnecessary to the process of collecting pertinent information. Efficiency rescues us. We have labels. Labels reproduce faster than rabbits or house cats, they insinuate content and they clarify such things as duty, power, authority or lack of, income brackets, skills, limitations, intelligence, talents, or education. They swiftly provide pertinent information.

"He's the banker." And the hearer nods "oh yeah," as if "the banker" is a term laden with common notions. As T. S. Eliot's Prufrock said, "There will be time, there will be time to prepare a face to meet the faces that you meet." Labels allow that split second needed for preparing a proper face. Some occasions require nothing more. But really discovering a person? Ah, that takes some lingering.

When a weekly woman's Bible study I taught grew to number several hundred, I met members through small casual gatherings. During one such occasion, I was caught up in conversation with a delightful young woman who after a few minutes smiled and said, "You remind me of our teacher."

I was dumbstruck. "Ahhh," I answered, "I *am* our teacher."

Now *she* was dumbstruck, as was the conversation. She apologized for not recognizing me and hastily explained that she sat at the back of the auditorium during class, "too far away to really see you." Regardless of my eagerness to continue, of our similarities, and the previous ease, the conversation ended. A label—The Teacher—did its job. A face met a face, but a person did not meet a person.

If we are courageous enough to discover that behind every label is an ordinary "I need food, comfort, encouragement, and a bathroom" sort of person, then intimidation by label ceases. Strangers, coworkers, family members, heroes, neighbors, or friends are people we can discover. Only we must dare a connection. We must stop the habit of hurry in order to show interest, to ask questions, to hear responses, to learn such things as

I didn't know you . . . collect baseball cards, rare
books, miniatures, hairballs or knitted caps . . .

I didn't know you actually like classical music, or
country music, jazz, blues, opera, rock . . .
that you ride your bicycle to work,
that you have such a sense of humor,
or three dogs and two cats,
or thirty outstanding parking tickets . . .

Aren't nearly as angry, bold, shy, serious, calm,
nervous, opinionated, tolerant, . . . as you appear

That you hate living here, love snow, miss childhood,
are energized by rain (me too),
buy everything on sale, bake bread, recycle,
never miss "The Simpsons," or "Nova," or both . . .

I didn't know you write poetry, speak four
languages, love science-fiction, hate to read,
or actually do read Keats, Fante, Updike, Kafka . . .
fear public gatherings,
are lonely, belong to that organization,
had/have cancer,
can't drive,
write letters to the editor,
Are a sports fan, opera fan, run the marathon,
paint, sing, build ultra-lites . . .

. . . Are single, divorced, married, widowed, a thinker,
feeler, poet, loner, mixer, adventurer, rebel, conformist,
extrovert, introvert . . . .

Not every connection is deep, but is at least real.

In *To Kill a Mockingbird*, twelve-year-old Jem was ordered by his father to spend a series of hours reading to old Mrs. Dubose. She was hateful, vindictive, insulting, and a lady.

"A lady?" asked Jem as his father broke the news of the woman's death. "After all those things she said about you, a lady?" His father replied,

> She was. She had her own views about things, a lot different from mine, maybe . . . son, I told you that [even] if you hadn't lost your head I'd have made you go read to her. I wanted you to see something about her—I wanted you to see what real courage is. . . . Mrs. Dubose . . . was the bravest person I ever knew.

Mrs. Dubose was a morphine addict who broke the habit before she died, but Jem did not know that, he only knew she was mean and intolerable. He needed to know better. Only by lingering, asking questions, by listening, observing, interacting, seeking truth and allowing surprise, by moving beyond labels, can we discover others.

If being real ourselves involves really knowing others (and I believe it does), and really knowing others involves some lingering but we prefer hurrying along with a collection of labels tucked under our arm, we need to ask why. One reason, at least, nearly knocks us over with its clarity: people lack curiosity about things they do not value, and, we must admit, there are many things we value above people. Things such as our emotional serenity, our privacy, our opinions, the opinion of others, our material security, our own labels, our time, a world of information.

The Problem: Value

A few summers ago I enjoyed a stay on the Hood Canal. I marveled at the occasional passing of a nuclear-powered Trident submarine, but even more, I was thrilled by the expanse of the Puget Sound in front of the house and a large, freshwater pond just behind it. At beach and pond I whiled away quiet hours with hot coffee and binoculars, watching an array of water birds. Day after day I avoided much of the writing work I came to do.

Then my friend Diane arrived. She is an Orange County business executive. She is as busy and bright as they come and not always interested in things that knock me over with joy. She and her husband, Tom, retreat to Palm Springs as often as time permits. They hit the latest movies, he golfs, she catches up on advanced computer literacy, reading, and journal writing. Diane hoped in Washington state to escape daily stress, to visit, to read, to take an occasional walk, but especially to avoid anything taxing . . . like bird-watching.

But my avid commitment to that exercise discomforted her (good). She reveled in the natural setting we shared but felt appropriate guilt (I helped) for neglecting the feathered crowd around us. She acknowledged the "darn" bird book. She adjusted the "stupid" binoculars and took an occasional glimpse. I was proud of her.

One morning the magic struck, and struck her hard. My city friend's excitement reached me as an eager and energetic whisper, "Barb! Come here, quick!" From the deck of our house, not more than eight feet from the tide's edge, her gaze was fixed on the railing of a neighbor's deck where a large bird was perched.

Cautiously pointing she whispered, "What kind of bird is *that?* It's hardly *moved* since I came out here!"

"Ah . . . Diane," I said carefully. Her enthusiasm was so genuine. "That's a wind sock."

"A *wind* sock?" The discovery enchanted her. "Is it *rare?*" she asked in awe.

"Diane, it's a *wind sock*," I said. "It's made of wood and canvas and turns freely on a post to tell you which way the wind is blowing. You know, a wind sock."

I lost control, roaring with laughter. Seeing the truth about her object of interest and waking from magic, Diane said, "Shoot! I was trying so hard to get into all this nature stuff. I really wanted to share your interest. Look what it gets me!" We were no longer being quiet, or moving carefully, or even interested in the bird on the neighbor's deck. It only became funnier. We were holding our sides, recovering. Our good humor was alive but our curiosity was not. Reality affects attitudes.

How on earth, in this demanding, threatening, fearful, overwhelming, exhausting, highly populated, and self-absorbed world, *how* can we get excited about people? Like wind socks, they continually turn in our space, swinging between foul and fair currents, announcing various perceptions of life. How do we remain curious about them when we have to work with them, worship and shop with them, compete with them; we see them on television, hear them on the radio; we are forced by media to know the world is full of all sorts of them; we wonder about them starving, or terrorizing, rebelling, snooping, or suffering. People worry us. We walk on sidewalks hoping they will not hurt us, rob us, or ask us to help them. We are overworked, overlooked, overruled, overwhelmed, or underrated by them. Even the people we call dear crowd our space, make too many demands, and drain our precious reserve of time and energy. Being too aware of too many people belongs to our generation, and the result is too often the death of curiosity and value. People are everywhere we turn, like zucchini in a never ending garden.

Solution: A Village View

When it comes to valuing others, surely it was more easily done when people lived in isolated villages, knew a small community well, and worried only to the edges of a square mile or two. That was enough.

Given the modern situation in which we are virtually forced to be globally aware, I think we must redevelop a village attitude. We must pull in our boundaries and unpeople our lives, generally speaking. Then we must tend a sensible space and wisely people our lives, specifically speaking.

Developing a village attitude for the sake of discovering others takes some lingering, a heavy dose of commitment, and some management of involvements and information. There is so much "out there" to do and know. To establish or to reexamine sensible boundaries, try lingering over questions like these:

• *What* do I actually need to know, or know about, in order to be a responsible citizen of my world, country, town, church, etc.? (Who can keep up with the daily onslaught of information! Limiting input is essential.)

• *Who* should I hear address subjects that interest me, or that I am responsible to; subjects that bring pleasure, growth, or opportunities for action? (I will learn about the upcoming school board election [ugh]; I want to hear about baseball and American history, yes, but I do not have to give a fig about details of the French Revolution, gourmet cooking, or how film is spliced.) It is a big job to limit input.

• *Where* do I waste too much time listening, working, or playing? How well do I balance activities?

• *Who* am I willing to hear that opposes my own views? (As much as I hate it, being real and especially being noble means being stretched and countered.)

Lingering over these questions helps us determine boundaries. Because opportunities are limitless, some deliberateness belongs to deciding which organizations to join or ignore, books to read, experts to hear, programs to take in, games to play, people to share time with, generally speaking. Real people say "no" to some things in order to say "yes" to better things—like discovering others.

Specifically speaking, discovering others involves abandoning abstractions about them. I am particularly fond of this currently popular abstraction: "Visualize world peace." My daughter and son-in-law have a bumper sticker that says, "Visualize whirled peas." I cannot help but wonder whether either exercise actually affects anything. I cannot help it, perhaps I should even apologize, but when I think of abstracting tendencies, I visualize a television evangelist who gazes from the screen and says to the world, "I love y-oo-u." I am mystified.

My mind responds, "Excuse me? You do not *know* me, let alone love me!" And, concerning the church, even we who are brothers and sisters in it frustrate the life out of one another in congregational meetings. We who do know and love one another can be observed refusing to serve on boards together; we feel good when we beat the other to the last parking place, and not even starlings can rattle their beaks better than we can cluck critical tongues toward the behavior of others' children.

I *know* what the TV preacher means. He does *not* mean "I love you," specifically. Rather, it is a general idea. A lovely one, an easy one because abstracted ideas are far easier to maintain than concrete relationships. It happens that, like many Protestant children, I grew up memorizing scripture. John 3:16 came along at about age five. I remember it this way: "For God so loved the world, that he gave his only begotten Son, that whosoever believeth in him should not perish but have everlasting life" (KJV).

I knew it well. Then, as unexpectedly as grease pops from bacon, one day I suddenly *heard* that verse. God so loved the world—this one, as it is not as it ought to be, not as it once was, or as it will be in God's time, but this as-it-is world. He so loved it that he *gave* concretely to it. Not platitudes or abstracted hope did He give. He gave directly, personally, his best. That, probably, is what love ought to cause us to do. But, we are not God. We are not able to value this world as admirably as does He.

Perhaps we can at least learn to better measure our language. What do we do with our expansive feelings of care? Globally speaking, we can locate and support any number of organizations that work to aid "the world." But, to *discover* others we must come home. Here, we need concrete behaviors and attitudes that connect with real people. Here, people have names. People in my village need food; some need comfort; some need to be heard or need to laugh. I can abstract all sorts of solutions for family disintegration occurring around the world, or I can take dinner to a neighbor who suffers the loss of job or a recent tragedy. The noble choice is hardly difficult to identify. Dostoyevsky nails it in *Brothers Karamazov* where a doctor says, "I love humanity, but I can't help being surprised at myself: the more I love humanity in general, the less I love men in particular . . . I mean, . . . as separate individuals."

Only God can actually love globally and particularly. For us, discovering others means lingering, locally. It means moving past labels. It means uncomplicating life enough to allow the value of a few to affect our attitudes and behaviors. There are a few people like Mother Teresa who set great examples of knowing globally but living locally. But she, and those like her, are different. Ahhh, my point exactly.

Lingering to Discover Ourselves

Our neighbor Karl is a biologist turned professional horticulturist. In a very few years he and his wife Helen turned their property into a priceless botanical garden. Often when my attitude sinks, I cross the drive and stroll through exotic plants, trees, and hothouses. Even Russian and box turtles live there. How grateful I am for it all.

Karl's plants come from around the world. One strange African succulent will never have more than the two thick, narrow leaves that now stick straight out of the ground. Only, if this fragile thing lives, in a matter of years its two leaves will stretch and spiral out, till they curl like the horns of a bongo, reaching their way to my house.

Karl's garden seems nearly perfect. But not everything in our little corner of the world is. He and Helen live in an inadequately small house. They compensate creatively, but, like ours, their house is old and needs constant repair. On this side of the drive our forty-some-year-old home has gradually and undeniably resigned to being a "fixer-upper." Everything cries for renewal, even the struggling fruit trees and the front-yard pansies. The massive silk oak, central to our front yard, oozes goo and threatens to up and die. Not even Karl wants to treat it.

We do not live in Eden, but the half-acre garden next door makes it seem that way. I touch, smell, stand back and admire rare living things. But Karl? When Karl walks with me, not only does he love the plants, he gives me details, Latin names, origins, histories, potentials, values. I have opinions; Karl has knowledge.

When it comes to "being," I hold opinions. There are experts who have knowledge. My geneticist friend explains being as a unique biological structuring of four simple molecules. By them, we are. Neurological researchers verify human being as a series of excited brain functions, while theologians posit talk about the image of God or a configuration of body, soul, and spirit. I wonder if linguists feel haughty when they calmly claim, "being is merely a state of existence." Some shove a stick in the spokes of their own discipline by suggesting that being requires conscious or moral awareness.

Major league philosophers examine being through ontological questions that belong to the discipline of metaphysics. They run along these lines: What is real? What is mere appearance? Is there reality beyond the things that are experienced through the senses? Are thoughts real? Is the mind real? Is time?

Some questions about being are asked by heavy-duty thinkers, but the author of this book is not one. I write about being like I walk through Karl's garden, an appreciator with opinions. I write concerning practical ontology. I hold and enjoy a gloriously naive opinion that we "are." "Are what?" Are free to commit ourselves to the development of noble character, an activity and a privilege only for people.

Dolphins, delightful though they are, cats, cunning though they be, cannot enjoy the high responsibility of developing character. *Noble,* as a descriptive word, may fit the instinctual manner of a Borzoi, but nobility is not an instinct; it is a choice about character belonging to people. Learned psychiatrists and philosophers can duke it out over why we are who we are, but I say, *since* we are, and since it matters, let us do something noble about it.

Discovering ourselves can mean many things, but on the popular level, at least, self-discovery usually refers to something psychological, romantic, or universally spiritual. Discussion of these subjects wins immediate and rapt attention. I wish my next topic were so generally fascinating. I rarely hear party conversation about it. I know few of my friends sit around addressing it, nor does it seem to play well on daytime TV. Its mention does not bring about astonishment, "Oh my goodness, yes!" or "I never thought about it, but boy, now that you say that . . ." My topic is a question: "What does it mean to live authentically in a technological society?"

One Possible Answer

Being real in the modern era requires living *in* but *against* technology. Saying that, I acknowledge the influence of French thinker Jacques Ellul. In the small book *Perspectives on Our Age,* he shows that technology is more than a phenomenon; it is a point of view. The undergirding of this strong assertion is this: Technology, he says, suppresses the subject. Right. That is, people are subjects. Things created by technology are objects. Imagine the surprise then when we realize that objects meant to free us from dreaded or difficult tasks have, in fact, become the merciless managers of people and their purposes.

For example, I once attempted in a lecture to clarify a point about technology's authority over us. I pointed to the lavaliere microphone I wore and said,

It does not matter who turns on a tape recorder. The subject of the task is inconsequential. It can be a child, a man, woman, an animal. The subject can be cruel or kind, tall or short. This is a technological moment. Not "who" but "that" it is done matters— and that it be done in accordance with the demands of technology.

Only then did I notice my failure to turn on the microphone when I began the lecture. The point was clear. The object suppresses the subject, and in this case, much of the subject's lecture.

You (subject) may care that a dog is struck down on a crowded highway, but your concern is secondary. The hurling vehicle (object) that saves you time and stretches your boundaries is primary. For good reasons, tons of metal moving you and many others to efficient ends cannot be subordinated to sudden feelings of sorrow or concern. The demands of the object rule the feelings of the subject. The object *is* the subject, I suppose we can say.

Unlike God or fellow human beings, technology requires nothing from the inside of us, from character. It demands only external disciplines—read the darned manual, learn how to push the right sequence of buttons, turn on the tape recorder before the lecture. If we are not careful, we run the risk of becoming like technology: efficient and impersonal.

My husband just called from upstairs, "Look out at the sky!"

"I see it," I yelled back. I work in front of a window, after all. But that was not good enough for him. I am instructed to get up, go outside, and look high in the darkening sky. (Mumble, mumble, he is always full of good ideas while I am trying to work.) Ah, the reward of cooperation! A stubborn wind shoves heavy, mottled clouds through the sky. The layer is low and looks every bit like the gray and black splotched coat of a seal. I have *never* seen clouds like this before. They are beautiful. Unlike my computer screen, also splotched with markings, technological markings, this touch of setting delivers a surge of joy. A split second of linger, a soaring spirit.

Technology is dumb to surges of joy. Computers and left turn arrows do not care who approaches; they do not care whether a machine's user has integrity. Do I? Do you? We all benefit from technology, but we must take care not to indiscriminately applaud it. It saves us time, and it relieves us of physical fatigue. But then it delivers us to mental and nervous fatigue. We moderns have the grand distinction of being stressed off the charts and of possessing the malaise, anxiety. Fear with reference to nothing. Don't applaud. Be wise and recognize that the age of technology is an age of self-doubt.

I am convinced that our generation is not nearly as self-indulgent as appearances suggest. Rather, we actively purchase and long to possess because we are sinking in self-doubt. What gives us value now, we who have abandoned time-honed human traditions and most physical labor? How do we sense worth, we who separate from generational homesteads and habits and need switches and cables to survive? Why with all our advanced products do people feel less safe, less satisfied?

Do not fret, says Advertising, today's handmaiden of technology. Are you lonely, sick, sexually dull, weary, overworked, unnoticed, unhappy, out of step? No reason to be. Consume, possess, purchase, gather gadgets, and the void you feel will be filled. In other words, let objects occupy you. See how well *things* fill voids, rule your time and mind. Every day there is a new model, a better distraction. Purchase, and you will feel good. How vulnerable we needy people are to the tinny voice of technology.

Technology boasts that we are freed from the rules of nature. How antiquated they were! We rarely notice great storms. We can watch television while they rage. We are seldom forced to rescue things from them, or to rest during them. We work at machines right through them, inside object-laden, storm-resistant buildings. We do not yield to sleep and solitude because of darkness; we turn on the lights and stay up around the clock. We even fight our wars in what once was figuratively called the dead of night.

We have technologically blighted the stars with our artificial light and canceled the sky's blue with technology's orange haze. We are no longer confined to a village. We travel around the world, euphorically suffering time zones and an aircraft's stale, recirculating air, seeing everything and knowing no place in particular. We do not have to die of disease; we now live miserably long in its company, beating it through technology that is bankrupting us.

On the lighter side perhaps, people of prosperous nations eat oranges year round, for technology has whipped the power of seasons. Of course, we no longer savor the smell of the peel, or pat the rare zest on our wrists. We do not appreciatively inspect the beautiful segments, or eat them slowly. Why should we? What is there to discover? Good question.

What is there to discover? Ourselves: who we have become or what we have ceased to be in this technological world. We must live in it, but to a character-saving extent we had better learn to live against it. By description, technology is artificial. It is wonderful, but it is artificial and can encourage us to be as well.

We may linger to discover ourselves on many levels, but this one is primary. We must pause where our sense of self meets the objects of our modern world. To be real means to be freed from the lie that a satisfied life depends upon appearances, possessions, purchase power. The difference between the manufactured appearance of a raspberry and a real raspberry makes me highly in favor of realities. A noble character is an internal reality not an external appearance. Its formation does not require things; it does not rise from them. It does require commitment.

Conclusion

Most people have heard the story about Jesus walking on water. The day it happened, in some deserted site near the Sea of Galilee, thousands of the curious and faithful had come to see him and hear him. They had mixed motives and broken bodies, and he had power. He healed them, fed them, taught them. He gave himself, locally.

Then, having sent his disciples rowing toward home, he managed somehow to "dismiss the crowd" and climbed a mountain for some private time of prayer. "When evening came" (he was a serious prayer), still standing on the hillside, he noticed the boat bearing his friends being battered by high waves. The disciples strained at the oars against an adverse wind, says Matthew's gospel. So be it. Jesus let them struggle till early morning when he walked toward them, on the water, and took care of the problem. That is the story in a nutshell. What is not in the nutshell is the remarkable addendum supplied by the gospel of Mark. "He intended to pass them by." What?

For hours Jesus kept an eye on those guys fighting mean

winds, stalled on the sea. Apparently he trusted their survival skills; they were fishermen, after all. In fact, he planned to pay no attention to them but to pass them by. Every writer has to cut something, but how Mark does tease our curiosity by his brevity. *Why* was Jesus intending to "pass them by"? Where was he going? What did he plan to do? What could be more important than the situation in front of him?

I have no authoritative answer, but I know this. In the midst of his intentions, contrary to set plans, Jesus lingered. He allowed himself to be distracted. Rarely will lingering seem to fit our schedules or intentions. Lingering results from paying attention to setting, to people, to ourselves. Beneficial lingering may require explanation, but it never calls for an apology. It is a must for real people. It is a pause, whether joyous or painful, by which we are always blessed.

CHAPTER
TWO

*L*istening

This is a true story and fitting, though perhaps not genteel. It began, "Charles Ray, are you *listening* to me?!" That was my mother's voice in the kitchen speaking harshly to my eleven-year-old big brother who was in some sort of trouble. His answer was "No, I'm listening to Granny." Our diminutive grandmother was also in the kitchen. She had just unintentionally but loudly passed gas.

The great sixteenth-century artist Benvenuto Cellini tells a similar story of listening to his friend Agnolo break the power of a dark and terrifying occasion when he "let fly such a volley from his breech that it was far more effectual than . . . asafetida." Forgive the pun, but listening is not a passive exercise. Often it is, as it was in these cases, a welcomed avenue to unimaginable relief. Listening is an exercise of hearing, but it is not to be confused with hearing.

Chuck heard our mother but was listening to Granny. Unless injury or a head cold prevents the normal course of things, we are always hearing. Three divisions of the ear, outer, middle, and inner, collect puffs of air (sound waves), whirl them through a coil or two, round the three smallest bones in the body, transform these pressure movements into electrochemical impulses, then shoot them a short distance along an auditory nerve through brain stem and mid-brain to the temporal lobe where, with the aid of Heschl's gyri, auditory reception is translated into perception. That is hearing.

Listening is selective and attentive hearing; the sort done by a French friend of ours who owns a recording studio. My husband, David, watched him perfect a German language radio commercial. He revised repeatedly. Listen, change, listen, retape, listen, sing, tape, listen. When Dave asked why such caution and care, Marc bared his great crocodile smile and said, "Beeg bucks!" There is no question about it: motivation improves listening.

Americans are motivated to pour "beeg bucks" into communication methodology, but more often than not that means speaking skills. We learn to verbally confront, convince, confuse, or confound. Speaking is important, of course. But whereas all forms of speaking tend to improve as people relax and situations become familiar, listening disintegrates in that same circumstance.

A long-term marriage, and may there be more of them, is a premiere example. Statistics and personal experience suggest the longer couples remain together the less likely they are to listen to one another. Why? It is proven that people predict the ideas of those they frequently hear. Our minds work much faster than our mouths, (we speak around 150 words per minute but we think between 600 and 1,200 words in the same period of time), so an undisciplined ear jumps ahead of a speaker. Like my somewhat-black lab who thinks she knows which direction we will go when I walk. She walks twice as far as our near-golden retriever, Ivy, who stays by my side. Storge doubles back, runs, doubles back, but never ceases to believe in her predictions. Goodness, by the time a verbalizer winds down, we hearers have circled round their thoughts three or four times, we have mentally finished for them and have practiced, at least once, the response we plan to the message we, ah, anticipated. As you might guess, this skill of neglect affects all forms of human cooperation: work, marriage, friendship, family. Unless we deliberately listen, we hear what we plan to hear and goodness knows where we wind up.

Tests that examine speech perception verify that when listening to a continuous speech pattern—that is, conversation as opposed to a list being read—people regularly hear sound that is not present. Just as the brain compensates for the blind spot that is before every human eye by finishing up visual pictures, the brain also makes major assumptions through our ears. How good of it.

To avoid a labyrinth of detail, in which I, too, get lost, may it suffice to summarize. Studies show we depend heavily upon the influences of our own grammatical and semantic context (inside our heads) in making decisions about what we perceive (from outside our heads). That is, our very mind's programming assists us in hearing assumptions rather than people. One researcher said people are "making good the inadequacies of what they hear." Is that a kind way of saying we prefer our own point of view?

I love it. We hear. We frequently do not listen. Realizing this, one might expect people to be concerned, to pay some "beeg bucks" for some listening skills. On the contrary, most of us prefer using our beeg bucks for hot fudge sundaes and cable TV. We contentedly maintain old, familiar patterns of response like: increased volume, increased emotional intensity, increased rejection of differing views, abrupt suspension of bothersome verbal exchanges, ridicule, red faces, red necks, red flags, put-downs, or flat denials. Perhaps you have noticed, few people listen well. But real people must.

Peripheral Silence—The Place of a Listener

I did some minor manuscript editing for a friend. She writes of a young couple who anticipated adoption of a foster child they cared for since its birth. By a cruel twist of judiciary processes, they lost the child and any hope of adoption. Their sorrow was beyond consolation. Consolation was poor. My friend asked the woman, "How do you wish people had responded to you in this crisis?"

She wished, she said, that people had listened. That they might have held back advice and "let me say what I needed to say." Instead, she was repeatedly told how to react. A good listener gets out of the center of things. Listeners must hear others accurately without immediately fixing, judging, correcting, or "making good the inadequacies." Listening is a noble activity that honors the voice of another. It is not a space in which we stitch together our responses. Listening requires our being peripheral people, being quiet while another speaks. It does not require agreement, only an active ear.

What seems like billions of years ago, I studied for a few weeks at L'Abri, a center for the investigation of Christianity located in the Swiss Alps. I was a young adult, and I was seriously questioning my faith. To wrap up study periods, evening discussions occurred around a crackling, warm fireplace. The particular night I remember, Udo Middelmann was taking questions. I asked one. It was unwieldy and involved a collection of clauses. Udo let me finish. He restated my question, confirming accurate comprehension, then he paused. I mean paused.

There was a silence so significant I felt I could hear it. Well before his answer began I learned something about people who listen. They enter the edge of a speaker's space. They allow silence. Listeners need it. I do not remember that particular question or its answer. I do remember hearing the pause, experiencing it in the midst of conversation. He suspended his own ideas and made room for the arrival of a message. Listeners work much like a baseball team's catcher. Catchers rivet their attention on the pitcher. The pitcher is the absolute center of things. Heaven help the team if the catcher grows bored by his own moment of inactivity and decides to practice signals while the pitch is sent.

I think of the majestic catch Jesus supplied when his opponents attempted to "catch Him in *His* words." Should they pay taxes to Caesar, they wanted to know. Having listened well, he put them to work and fired back a question. They brought him the requested coin and acknowledged that Caesar's image was pressed upon it.

Then, he suggested, the answer is easy. Give to Caesar what belongs to him. By the way, he added, give to God the things that are God's. "They marveled at Him," I read in Mark 12. Well, so do I. A coin bears the Caesar's image but the image of God is pressed onto humanity. For anyone listening, the message is profound: give to God that which bears his image—ourselves. By listening well, Jesus left the conversation where it belonged. Not with the victory in a battle of words but with the power of a proper response.

I am still moved by the memory of Udo solidly catching my question and sending back an appropriate response. Good listening is a powerful skill and a gift to any who receive it. It is also a discipline of noble character. It is rare, excellent, and responsible. Respect for the opinions and thoughts of others comes from inside a person whose values stretch beyond themselves, whose attitudes and behaviors demonstrate concern.

Pitcher's Mound Mentality

I am convinced that most people fail to listen for one simple reason: they are busy talking to themselves. If a catcher stands on the pitcher's mound, even if he is shaping brilliant, powerful signals there, he is working from the wrong place. A "listener" who stands on a speaker's story, working in their own head on personal and powerful responses, is like that. No outside voice can be pitched to them. They are in the wrong place. They hear but do not listen. They are mentally pitching their own thoughts rather than catching the thoughts of another. In either instance, the game is not worth attending.

In chapter one I suggested that we are not nearly so self-indulgent as we are sufferers of self-doubt, and now I propose that we are not nearly so selfishly self-centered in conversation as we are insecurely so. Insecurity accounts for a vast amount of personal preoccupation. It constantly fidgets over the shape and seams of our appearance. An insecure person never feels quite properly suited up. Everyone else looks comfortably outfitted in what we wear poorly: esteem, confidence, right answers, popularity, impressionability. I do not know if impressionability is a word, but I know that it says what I mean. Insecurity encourages us to worry about an impression of presence rather than to be authentically present. People living real lives have finished fidgeting; they are authentic. Not faultless, not perfect, not of superior intelligence, just unself-consciously aware of who they are.

Like Shirley. I met her in Okinawa where our husbands were based as fighter pilots. Together we played bridge, sang in a wives club choir, attended Bible study, endured pregnancies, and tried to learn what it meant to be an Air Force officer's wife. We learned quickly that it meant different things to different women. I can tell you what it meant to Shirley.

One Sunday she and Dick invited a few couples to their house for dinner after church. When we walked in, Shirley said with a musical voice, "Take your shoes off, make yourselves comfortable. I am a preacher's kid, and the Lord knows we at least need Sunday as a day of relaxation. Besides, I wouldn't even know how to work up an air of formality." She served up a wonderful day.

I marveled at this woman's self-confidence and genuine ease, which, of course, she immediately passed on to her guests. When Shirley listens she listens like Jesus, like Udo. She grabs contact with your eyes, stays in the catcher's box, remains silent while you pitch from the mound, and considers it her job to catch whatever you send to her.

Self-Check

Why is it so hard to listen to others? What is it we are doing while others speak? We are talking to ourselves, practicing signals. I call it, "self-checking." Self-checking is a preoccupation by which we assure ourselves that we are who we thought we were when we last checked. Children are great at it, till they grow aware of observers. Their open fascination with reflected images of themselves delights us all. Adults are nothing short of comedic in their discreet attempts of self-checking.

Ever notice someone walking by a large expanse of glass? First comes a posturing, appearing to observe something through the glass. We self-checkers feign great disinterest, but by our contorted efforts to case our own reflection, we resemble an Egyptian art figure, body presenting itself fully to the outside but face in profile. Adults do not blatantly stare. We self-check in nanosecond glances, artistically.

What is that great assurance that sweeps over us in self-check? "Yep, I'm okay." We long for it, even if it results in a negative reassurance. "Yep, it is as bad as I thought, the run is still in my stocking" or "I'm still short."

We live our whole lives with ourselves yet never seem adequately acquainted. It is as if each morning we rise, look in the mirror and say, "Oh yes, there I *am*. I am real. I am who I thought I was. I am glad to see me again." Self-check is a strong, natural, and constant urge, but if it is not subdued in the company of others, it subverts authentic human connection.

Not only do we visually self-check; we also self-think. In fact, it has been suggested that about 90 percent of all thought is self-thought. Without discipline, this is what it does to us. While others speak, our mind works to decide whether we agree, what we would have done in their situation, especially how this information will affect us, how we feel about it, and how we feel they should feel. Most detrimentally, while they speak we plan our reply. We move from the catcher's box up to the mound and practice signals during a strike-zone pitch. We *are* hearing them, but we are listening to ourselves. Not so noble. People wanting to connect authentically with others must control the annoying habits of self-think, self-check. How wonderful, really, to take a break; to escape that 90 percent preoccupation. But how? By playing a game.

Tetherball Method of Listening

It helps me considerably to picture all informal conversation as a tetherball game. Normally, a tetherball is attached by a rope to a central pole. When I was a kid, players squared off and socked that ball back and forth. Pace and strategy can change, but the same ball is played. Picture such a pole as conversation, but imagine three ropes with three differently colored balls attached, waiting for play. As the listener, pay close attention to which ball sails your way, then send that ball back when your turn comes. You will get a chance to serve, to initiate play, but not now. That's a new game.

Unless talk is punched into a discussion of abstractions, all conversations volley one of these three topics: *experience, behavior,* or *feelings*. These are the balls of the game. They are not the same color, they do not sound the same as they whip around the pole, and they do not play alike. Your job? Identify the ball the speaker plays and send it back.

When people speak of experience they share something that happens to them. It may be an experience you can picture, an open act. Ice skaters Kurt Browning of Canada and Christopher Bowman of the USA might like to tell you about the experience of being in the 1992 Olympics, of trying to complete a triple axle jump followed by a triple toe loop. Or they may talk about how their hearts were beating inside their chests right before going onto the ice. They experienced that, too, but you cannot see it; it is a concealed experience. *Experience: things that happen to people. Some are obvious, some are concealed.* Color experience red. But wait. Maybe these incredibly talented and trained men want to talk about what they *did* when it came time for the axle jump. You cannot see that Christopher told himself, "Do it! Do it right!" but he can tell you about his concealed behavior. Or he may describe obvious behavior, "Did you notice me bite my tongue on takeoff?" Imagine behavior as a yellow ball ready for play. *Behavior: things people do or refrain from doing, openly or not.*

"Do you want to know how I felt when I missed that first combination jump?" Kurt may ask. Immediately you know a new ball is in play, say, a blue one. *Feelings: how people are affected by things, especially by behavior or experience.*

Since in personal conversation there are usually only three topics to expect, your work is simply to pay attention to which ball is coming your way. You do not tell people which ball to begin with or how to deliver it. In a negative sense, listening means not playing both sides of the pole.

Listening means getting yourself out of the center of things. It means noticing the people who speak to you. Pay attention to what happens while they talk. Catch their mood, the color of the conversation. Is it frivolous or frantic? Are they reluctant or eager players? Do they need to attack, or always win, or are they here to play fair, to exchange thoughts? Are they afraid of the game? Are they self-conscious? Those conditions of play help you frame responses.

Perhaps nothing intrigues me more concerning conversation than the frequency of the phrase "I just don't know what to say." I have said that often enough, when anticipating an introduction or entering a new situation. How odd that we hesitate, as if some scripted version of good or appropriate communication is out there somewhere like a floppy disk, ready to insert prior to opening our mouths. Responses are just that, responses to situations already in play. They are not required, dreadful tasks. But, since they often seem so, the pain of them lessens when a few techniques are applied.

Our verbal responses are the pertinent return of three topics served us: experience, behavior, and feelings. Real people reply authentically but attentively. Topics are limited, but we have unlimited ways to play them. One of the best? The question mark slammer.

"How did it *happen*—this experience, this behavior, this feeling? What did you *do* about how you *felt?* How mad was that guy in that *experience?* What did you *do* next? What did you *think?* Oh gosh, how did you *feel* when you saw that, or did that, or heard that?" So far you have played a basic game. No conversational finesse has even been tried, for goodness sake. The opportunity to add details and descriptions of feelings, place, things, ideas, is yet to emerge. A finesse is an enhancement, a great quote, an example out of history or memory, a question about a fine point alluded to but not yet explored. When those touches are added, good conversation leaps to greatness and can play through the night. Listen for the opportunity to finesse, but start at the first level of play where you gain a confidence of response.

Did conversation send you a red ball? Send it back with a question attached. When listeners talk they ask questions. When people slap a topic into conversation, they are signaling a readiness to discuss it. It is harder for some than for others, but still we know that people love to talk about themselves. Nothing is kinder than to be asked a question that grants permission to keep talking. Rest assured. People mention subjects they want to discuss. Do them a favor. Stay on target, volley the subject they served you, ask for more. Questions come easily when we intend to learn rather than instruct.

What does listening take? The answer is a question: Do I choose to hear another accurately, or do I prefer hearing myself working on my judgment and response?

We Have Nothing to Fear But Hear Itself

A few years ago, as I was finishing up my seminary degree, I served on a ministerial search committee. One evening over dinner, the committee interviewed a fine man. True, his opinions about women's service to the church differed drastically from mine, but, heck, I was idealistic and optimistic. I had seen many people, including pastors, move from narrow ideas about women to adopt kinder, more tolerant views. Surely, it could be done again.

As I ate delicious, garlicky pasta, a fellow committee member asked our prospective candidate, "Barb here will soon graduate from seminary. How will you use her in the church?" The candidate admitted this was a problem; he was honestly unsure. I dedicated my gaze to serious pasta picking. Here we go again, I thought. He appreciated my training but felt firmly that Scripture prohibits female leadership, generally speaking.

Now this was a nice guy. He had a good sense of humor and an easy style of communication. He was likable and had a great wife. So even as he talked I took heart, believing there was room down the road for dialogue. I said, "I know that we stand poles apart on the subject of what women can do in the church, but I just wonder if you are open to discussion on the matter?"

"When you ask that," he responded, "if you mean, can you come into my office and talk about the issue, of course. If you mean, will I change my mind? Never."

And do you know what? He was right. I did, and he did not. Now, this is not pastor-bashing time. This good man is not my subject. Well, that is not entirely fair to say. I *meant* for this man to be my subject. I meant to say that his reaction exhibited a common human tendency: to hear rather than listen. But as he and I talked about my printing this story, I suddenly faced a new slant. That of my own behavior.

How noble of me, really, that in that old meeting strong with garlic and differing points of view I wanted him to listen to me. The truth is, I wanted him to *agree* with me. I heard him, I knew his doctrinal position well. I grew up with it after all; by, in, under, and finally, mostly against it. But while I wished his view were more expansive, I also wished not to alter my own. He heard. I heard. But who listened?

I very much wanted to write about *his* closed mind. Only, in review, I am confronted by my own. The only comfort to me is that the potential for a closed mind is virtually epidemic. Who has not realized that once convinced of something—even justifiably convinced—we frequently stop testing and start guarding our view.

With the exception of a very few moral absolutes, most ideas deserve polishing. If they are overly protected from the rub of influence, we have likely moved from the position of a good mind to that of a closed mind. Like a New York City shop on Columbus Avenue with bars drawn across the windows and door, that mind is well-stocked, it is safe, but it is closed. Hearing is safe. But if we hope to listen, we have nothing to fear but "hear" itself.

Mortimer Adler, editor of *Encyclopaedia Britannica*, lecturer, philosopher, and author of as many thoughtful books as there are rings on a healthy tree, points out this: When headlines about international dialogue read, "CONVERSATION DETERIORATING," we begin to worry. "NEGOTIATIONS COMPLETELY BROKEN DOWN," alerts us to the probability of war. In other words, the absence of dialogue is an absence of hope.

How perfectly officials of the U.S. State Department demonstrated Adler's point on the eve of the Persian Gulf war. Just before flying off for "talks" with Iraq, one negotiator, waving goodbye and flexing national resolve, said, "We will talk, but we will not compromise." Translated: "We will hear but not listen."

Pardon me? Before we even begin, we *plan* mental deafness? Who is surprised (whether or not warranted, I am no expert on international negotiations) that our headlines soon ran, CONVERSATIONS COMPLETELY BROKEN DOWN. Talk, yes. Hear, yes. Listen? Not at all. Please note, when listening is neglected and hearing is the planned response, talk is always personally safe, and perfectly predictable, but fruitless. Not so noble, not so good.

Too often potential conversational conflict is approached like a petty dictator protecting his domain. Closed minds and closed-minded rulers both suffer a certain paranoia. Someone is always out to "get" them. Opinions outside an approved party line are considered inflammatory; they set off alarm systems and frantic defense troops rush to quell the riot. Petty dictators and closed minds both expel offenders. They threaten and cry "poor me" when opposed.

No, I do not fear information "out there" threatening our precious opinions nearly as much as I do the absence of a listening ear in our families, marriages, friendships, communities, churches, and schools. To "hear" where "listen" belongs, worries me. It is "hear" itself we need to fear. Listening dialogues, and without it nothing is left but isolation, animosity, or war. A real person strives for excellent comprehension, not victory, welcomes the experience of learning, and safely connects with other imperfect people. Rare, true, but noble.

A Little "Listen" Lesson

In a Listen and Learn tape obtained from a public library, Dr. Adler cites a Sperry Corporation study. Of the four basic language skills, adults use 46 percent of their time *listening*. Of course, it is the first of all language skills used. In infancy we hear symbols, tone, style of language. Later, we learn to speak. Some say our first words mimic our oldest idea of language, the heartbeat, Ma-ma, Da-da, ya-ya, thump-thump.

Speaking, once mastered, requires 30 percent of our time, *reading*, if we still do that, uses about 15 percent of an adult's time, and *writing*, that venue schools require us to practice more than any of the rest, occupies only 9 percent of an adult's time. Listening comprises 46 percent of our language work. How many listening lessons do you remember?

I cannot forget an early and most indelible one that came my way in Naha, the capital city of Okinawa. In this case a fellow Air Force wife was my instructor, and it happened in a small company of women shopping. In fact, if I could return to an unchanged Naha, lo, these many years since 1961, I could identify the broken spot of sidewalk where my eyes fell and burned while that gentle woman's lesson struck. It was a doozy. Not deliberately but definitely. Lisa wearied of me. Her real name was not Lisa, but she *was* a few years my senior and really very many years wiser.

I was twenty-one. I was a happy, multidimensional (read unfocused) woman with one infant son. My vast experience included approving parents, fun, high school, one semester of college, major ice skating, and marriage at age eighteen. Not much had come along yet to knock some me out of me. As our group talked through the Naha morning, I failed (they did not) to notice that every story they told reminded me of one of my own. Down to the proper storage of furs, I contributed my memories, my advice, my opinion, my expertise, my slant, my broad knowledge. I was having a wonderful time, conversing, hearing, listening—listening? Then came the lesson. Quiet, lovely Lisa told a story that, naturally, reminded me of something I should contribute. I jumped to edit her conclusion. How good of me. She started to rebut. Then, piercing me with the sharpness and accuracy of her assessment and her dark eyes, she said, "Oh, that's right. I forgot, you know everything."

What I knew mostly was that at that moment I needed to evaporate. It would have been a mercy, really. I was pinned to the obvious as surely as an insect is pinned in a collector's glass case. I "heard" in order to speak. I did not listen. I rarely moved out of the center of things. I did not bother to catch. I did not know to hit the ball back to a speaker, or to ask questions about them, to encourage their story to grow and unfold because I got genuinely absorbed in it. I was a master at self-check. I thought every story reflected my own image. My attitude and behavior announced that. I made myself the subject of every conversation . . . even though that had not consciously occurred to me. I needed Lisa that day. I wish she had been less accurate for my ego's sake, but my growth needed the lesson she stuck through my heart.

Conclusion

Several years ago, a large opportunity arrived in our small town. A noted Catholic priest accepted a challenge from a local fundamentalist clergyman to debate the inspiration of Scripture. David and I decided to attend. We arrived as an explanation of formal debate was concluding.

The local minister approached the podium to present his argument, and we slipped into the back row of seats. A hundred or more people sat between us and an excellent presentation. Both speakers did well. They respected debate rules, they were prepared, poised, and powerful throughout presentations and rebuttal. I was glad to have come. The Bible-schooled fundamentalist held his own beautifully against the scholarly Jesuit.

He did, but his people did not. They held their own till room lights lifted and questions were permitted from the floor. Not even a bright room dimmed the powerful wattage of opposition burning in this crowd. How proud they were of their secure tenets. How ready they were with barbed and pushy questions, the sort that say, "Whadya think about that one, buddy, huh, huh? Gotcha, huh?" It became quite clear that every question was a trap. Yes! Yes! their postures and voices signaled, let us defeat this calm scholar.

I do not remember a single inquiry that concerned his stated position, not a question that required a defense of his argument. There were plenty about his eternal security, about his Roman view of truth. But even those were rhetorical. He was not questioned; he was on the rack of a fundamentalist inquisition. And let me tell you, these people were good at it. I felt like someone secretly rolled a Woody Allen movie and that soon we would all start laughing at the not-so-subtle joke before us. This was one, wasn't it?

It was not. I do not know if the priest had any supporters there, but clearly perfected Protestants came en masse to lynch a Catholic priest and vindicate the Lord. A fine debate fell under foot, trampled by Christian storm troops. My emotions smoldered in sorrow and rage. Largely, I suppose, because I was raised under fine fundamental teaching. These people spitting anger and pride were, somehow, my people. They were emotionally over an edge. Of course, so was I. I clutched the edges of my seat and worked against fury. Fortunately, shock held me motionless.

The guest, the pariah, the unacceptable man of the collar, kept cool. And then it was over. But for exiting self-congratulatory chatter, it was over. I sat, watching the saints file out. The speakers were at the front of the room receiving people. I spoke briefly to the fundamentalist; then the priest and I shook hands.

"I need to say how sorry I am for the way you were treated here tonight," I said. "Theologically, I am related to this audience, but I am grieved by their behavior. I truly apologize."

He took my hands in his and patted out comfort. "Oh, my dear," he said kindly. "Don't worry for a moment about me. You know, you just learn to expect this sort of behavior from this kind of people."

This kind of people? Sadly, he was right. "CONVERSATION DETERIORATING, WAR LIKELY." This group rightly defended a position. Rightly, perhaps, but not nobly. They proved bold but not admirable. They heard but were not listening. Listening is an art perfected by people who accept voices other than their own, who catch well, who correctly interpret signals sent by another.

CHAPTER
THREE

*L*earning

It matters little to the overall shape of things in the world that I know barnacles stand on their heads and eat with their feet. But I can tell you that it makes a great difference to me when I stoop at ocean's edge and see them feed. What a delightful moment. Pleasure is immediate when I watch their fern-like feet search the shallow water for food. I feel like God has let me in on a private joke. I am glad I learned about barnacles.

It matters little to the overall shape of things in the world that I learned about the mitochondrion. This is not a medieval town; it is a hungry little sausage-shaped entity living in eucaryotic cells (the sort we are made of) and is a biological miracle. I understand that, technically speaking, miracles do not visit biology. Still, this seems like one.

Imagine one of your own cells pumped up to 100,000 times its normal size. Toss this six-foot pulsing membrane out on the lawn, watch how it works, continually changing shape, bulging here and snapping back there, oozy but contained by its thin, outer membrane. Watch your foot—a cell eats nearly everything within reach! Inside that enlarged cell you can see a colony of fifty to five thousand mitochondria.

Like all bacteria, the submicroscopic mitochondrion originally lived in the air, was driven by a voracious appetite, and regularly leapt onto things (like our teeth) to feed. Uncontrolled, nothing was safe in its company. Not even a mutually hungry single cell. Consequently, says biologist Lynn Margulis, a prehistoric deal was struck, a beneficial one.

Mitochondria were invited by life processes to live inside all cells with a nucleus. They agreed not to eat their hosts as long as cells agreed to provide a constant supply of food. Fair enough. Working at a 50 percent efficiency level, mitochondria pods surrender to the host cell all the energy produced by their mighty munching. By that energy, all forms of life are animated.

"And they lived happily ever after." Mitochondria dart about and feed in cytoplasmic currents like my stubborn old goldfish, Sartre, swims and feeds in his aquarium. Thanks to the cooperative venture between cells and mitochondria, corn grows, fish swim, frogs leap, and human high jumpers make it over the bar. Only it should not be so.

My attention was seized by this news one day as I skimmed books about cells. I was looking for information about the brain but fell across the fact that the mitochondrion has its own DNA. This is as unlikely as saying human beings live well on the ocean floor. Impossible. I kept reading. I lingered. I learned.

DNA, the blueprint for life, consists of four chemical molecules that, depending upon their coded arrangement, turn out beach grass, warthogs, college professors, or land crabs (which once marched as an army across southern Florida from the Atlantic, through my garage, to the Gulf of Mexico). DNA never equivocates. It can be defective, but it does not equivocate. Setting different codes for every single living thing, DNA then safeguards each arrangement against the intrusion of any other. Mitochondria break the rule.

In the case of humans, every cell (trillions for each of us) holds in its nucleus forty-eight chromosomes that house about three thousand genes each. Every gene holds a yard's worth of two carefully twisted spaghetti-like strands coated with the billions of chemical bits mentioned above, DNA. Oh, yes, that "yard's worth" of stuff packed in a gene is equivalent to "30 miles of gold thread stuffed into a cherry pit," says geneticist John Medina in his book *The Outer Limits of Life*. Every living entity has its own and *only* its own DNA. That is the law of life.

Now enters our submicroscopic, sausage-shaped, energy-producing organelle: the mitochondrion. What business does it have in corn, cattle, or your cells when its blueprint disqualifies it? The DNA of mitochondria resembles hula-hoops, not our twisted spaghetti stuff. It carries along a complicated biological story of a female transmitted part of you that is absolutely essential but technically, uh, not you. The rules crumble. Mitochondria with its own DNA, ignores all "No Trespassing" signs, climbs the fence, grazes in all living things, and sets us in motion. Technically, it should not. It does avoid bacteria and some forms of algae, but otherwise it lives in and animates all else.

It matters little to the overall shape of things in the world that I read about mitochondria. But it matters tremendously to me. Learning even as little as I have about it, I sense the wonder of being, the miracle of animation, the unexpected flexibility of biology, the privilege of a mind.

Learning is to us what the mitochondria is to the eucaryotic cell—that is, it is energy and vitality, surprise and necessity. *What* we learn about things, ideas, people, sports statistics, the golden mean, or the making of tofu is not nearly as important as *that* we learn; that we *acquire knowledge or skill by study, instruction, or experience.* If we commit ourselves to being real, that is, authentic, mentally and emotionally energized, safely connected to others in our world, sensitive to the moment, and moved by solid values, we will need to know that learning matters. And, I believe, by instruction or experience we must learn at least these three things:

- Leisure is work worth doing.
- Ignorance is a self-imposed prison.
- Life is always a lesson, whether or not we learn it.

Leisure Is Work Worth Doing

Some things I understand so slightly that it is best that I say little about them. Aristotle, for example. I know he was amazingly well-educated and that he influenced nearly everything (natural history, politics, physics, theology, art, physiology, ethics, astronomy, philosophy, for starters), that he is the father of Western logic, that his teacher was Plato (whose great systems he discarded), and that his own famous student was Alexander the Great (who successfully ignored much of his master's advice).

My reading of Aristotle begins and ends with a few pages from his Nichomachean Ethics. An eye dropper could suck up my grasp of Aristotle and still have space in it. But, oh, what a precious few drops I have. From Aristotle I learned a lesson on leisure.

Time, says Aristotle, should hold two serious forms of work.

First, *subsistence work*. That is, any sort of utilitarian job we do or hope our children will get and hope earns them enough pay to allow for basic needs—shelter, food, and a VCR.

Then, time is used for what the great philosopher called *leisure work*. Leisure, he said in the second century B.C., consists of moral work, the training of mind and spirit in such things as religion, ethics, art, and science. Leisure is a job, a discipline, not a measure of free time, not a means of income. Artistotle called leisure "work," and he called a job "work," then the relief from these two things he called "play."

Is it easy? Is it fun? These are good questions to ask but not about work, only about play. We play, goof off, and get silly in free time, but free time is not leisure time. The distinction is crucial. Jobs we understand; play, too, but what is leisure? My dictionary says leisure is "freedom from demands of work or duty."

Aristotle would say, "Fie!" (Would a Greek say "Fie"?) Surely Aristotle says, "Not on your life!" *Leisure is not a state of being free from demands, not a noun, not an adjective describing time, not play. Leisure is work, a commitment to activity whereby fine character is built.* I like that. But, when Aristotelian categories evaporate, as they have of late, where then do we place the task of developing character? Is it play? It is not. Is it a job for which we are paid and by which we subsist? It is not. In our modern era when time is regularly sliced in two, like a sandwich, where fits leisure, the work of building noble character?

When do we train the mind and spirit? When do we learn to be fine people? It concerns me that the word *fine* regularly describes music or art but rarely people. Fine is not limited to a critic's vocabulary, it does not equate to snobbery, and it is not a station in life. It is a sum of money imposed as a penalty but not only that. It is an unlabeled French brandy but not only that. Fine still means of superior or best quality. Fine fits construction workers, homemakers, engineers, loggers, and IRS agents. Well, maybe not IRS agents. Fine people work two jobs and relieve both with play. It is good to learn that time well used coils like three tightly woven strands of rope: job, leisure, and play.

Leisure trains and exercises attitudes and behaviors. Its work is to shape fine human character. It requires a commitment of time and an aim toward nobility. As a Christian, I cannot help but enjoy imagining a congregation's response to someone calling Bible study a "leisure" activity. "What will it be today? Golf? A walk in the woods? Bible study?"

But is there a finer example of Aristotle's leisure than that which comes from the apostle Paul to the Philippian Christians? Learn to look for at least one of these qualities in every situation you experience, in every person you meet, in every task you approach (even rotten experiences permit at least one—just keep looking). This is work. This is leisure.

> whatever is true, whatever is honorable, whatever is just, whatever is pure, whatever is pleasing, whatever is commendable, if there is any excellence and if there is anything worthy of praise, think about these things. Keep on doing the things that you have learned. (Philippians 4:8–9 NRSV)

Lee Atwater, former George Bush campaign manager, at age forty lay dying of a brain tumor. He said, "My illness helped me to see that what was missing in society is what was missing in me—a little heart, a lot of brotherhood . . . and to see that we must be made to speak to this spiritual vacuum at the heart of American society, this tumor of the soul" (*Time*, May 10, 1993).

Believe it or not, leisure is meant to make us see such things. If we begin to live the leisurely life early enough, our regrets will be narrowed. "Think about these things . . ."

Ignorance Is a Self-Imposed Prison

It was a surprising thing, my earning a graduate degree in theology. Since I did not fulfill the seminary's entrance requirements, I was admitted on probation. But admitted I was. Regardless of the passage of time and the lifting of probation, the first few days of every quarter roused in me two reactions. I was thrilled by the privilege of school. Then hot on the heels of joy came fear. "This class is my Waterloo. The holes in my knowledge are massive. Here, in this class, I will fail."

With good reason I felt that way the first day of Dr. Dan Fuller's class, Unity of the Bible. He explained to the hundred or so students seated in lecture rungs that our grades depended greatly upon understanding Jonathan Edwards's publication, "A Careful and Strict Inquiry into the Modern Prevailing Notions of that Freedom of Will, Which is Supposed to be Essential to Moral Agency, Virtue and Vice, Reward and Punishment, Praise and Blame."

Well, hey, I knew I was in trouble. I was unacquainted with Jonathan Edwards, knew nothing about his writings, could hardly follow the Title of the Treatise Let Alone Plumb Its Depth, but knew somehow in his ideas was vested my GPA. So when the professor invited questions, I said, "I may be the only one here who needs to ask this, but just who is Jonathan Edwards?"

The class cracked up. Funny was not what I meant to be,

but apparently during the years I spent raising children my scholarly classmates (a great group of kids) had armed themselves with complete knowledge. For whatever reasons, they found my ignorance amusing. Maybe, I think, just maybe they made a mistake we all occasionally do make, confusing ignorance with stupidity.

Mine was a question of ignorance, but it was not a stupid question. It was not that I was incapable of learning about Mr. Edwards; it was only that, as yet, learn I had not. Ignorant I was, *lacking in knowledge or training*. Stupid I was not, *lacking ordinary keenness of mind, mentally dull*. Ignorant I often find myself; ignorant I do not have to remain. Or, I *can*. Some things I cannot or do not want to know. Fortunately, Dr. Fuller respected my question, briefly introduced Jonathan Edwards (I was not the only class member taking notes, I noticed), and whetted my appetite for the task ahead.

I happily report earning an A in that class, and one on the difficult paper concerning Jonathan Edwards. Not too many people did. I admit I never really understood the theology of Edwards, but, studying him, I learned other things. I learned about eighteenth-century America, the Great Awakening, religion of the heart; about smallpox and a new vaccine for it from which a brave Edwards died. I learned of a gentle man with imposing ideas.

Ignorance is a self-imposed prison, or it is only a bog to step through in a rutted field of learning. Many conditions of life are unavoidable, but ignorance is not one of them. I venture that if we choose to remain ignorant by avoiding information or questions that free us, then either fear or conceit rules our hearts. Interestingly, the motive of fear and conceit is often the same. Looking informed wins out over being informed. Appearances concern us more than realities. Knowing and learning matter less than seeming and feigning. It takes courage to live fully. It takes learning.

So let us say our courage wins. We energetically slosh through the bog of ignorance, and we escape our self-imposed prison. We are learning. Suddenly, we face a new trap ignorance sets: the strong jaws of certitude. Certitude knows. It is not fact necessarily but it is freedom from doubt. It does not say, "I am convinced" or "I think." It insists and says, "I know and I am right." It frames certainty, hangs it on a "think no more" wall of the brain, and shields it from any incursions of doubt. Certitude imprisons growth.

The truth is, to some degree, we all enjoy what Reinhold Niebuhr called "standpatism." It feels good to think you know, absolutely. It fosters security. And arrogance, I fear. Certitude seldom concerns itself with noble character. It concerns itself with winning arguments and avoiding different points of view. It concerns itself with being right.

Perhaps certitude, standpatism, exists legitimately in mathematical equations, or in the declaration that water is wet or that humans are not sea gulls. But beyond physically verifiable facts, knowledge is at its best when tempered by humility and appropriate doubt. In fact, learning requires the suspension of certitude and the presence of doubt.

Doubt is not cynicism, and it is not skepticism. It is a means of testing beliefs and opinions. It is a route to accuracy. Like fire to iron, it tempers, shapes, strengthens our thoughts. In truth, not knowing is seldom the problem for most of us; the humility of not knowing is. Perhaps that is most difficult for those of us who are deeply religious people. People who feel certain they know.

Strong faith, we must learn, is not necessarily good faith. Human certainty is not what God requires of us concerning

Him. God is his own unwavering measure. We are people, desiring to believe rightly and well. We may defend God's existence, but we are not proofs of it. We are benefactors. *Faith and certitude are not synonyms*. Faith, by its very definition, means trusting without having all the evidence to justify trust. In *The Clown in the Belfry,* Frederick Buechner writes that "Faith is a way of seeing in the dark." We are in the dark, he says. "And God knows, the dark is also in us." No wonder faith is a matter of benefit and of humility. Faith has room for doubt. Certitude has too often shaded the Light meant to guide faith.

"The crusades were carried out in virtuous bad faith," wrote novelist Umberto Eco. How I wish he were wrong. Speaking of later centuries, Reinhold Niebuhr said, "We fair-minded Protestants cannot deny . . . that it was Protestantism that gave birth to the Ku Klux Klan, one of the worst specific social phenomena which the religious pride and prejudice of peoples has ever developed" (Richard Fox, *Reinhold Neibuhr*). I wish he were not so accurate. I wish the white Protestant church, the parent of my own faith, had swallowed a small dose of doubt to cure its devastating certitude.

Learning does not suggest abandoning deep beliefs. It only means being courageous enough not to confuse them with concrete, courageous enough to test them, courageous enough to be wary of certitude. Religious people are not the only people to believe deeply and cherish stubborn opinion, of course. Self-imposed prisons of opinion collect all sorts of characters.

I write in an election year. Even in the early days of campaigning, candidates produced political certainties enough to wallpaper the White House brown. Slogans and speeches flung certitude everywhere, hoping ignorant voters would remain so. Whereas, testing promises, protests, and assertions of even our favorite political people could summon greater integrity from them. Loyalty—political or otherwise—is not a commitment to ignorance of all but your own point of view. Loyalty is good but it *is not a synonym for certitude*, although if you stumbled onto a discussion of politics by my redheaded uncles and aunts you would say it is. Or you would think so if my late grandfather, Pop, were your counsel. He, in two or three colorful sentences, solved the problems of our nation by sinking one political party and anointing the other. Loyalty? Commendable. But "Why loyal?" is an important question to ask if we hope to avoid a prison of ignorance.

Most forms of certitude rise above reason. Immovable idealism does. Faith systems and politics can produce this tendency, but nothing demonstrates this form of certitude better than young couples during the last trimester of a first pregnancy. Impending parenthood can call up certitude as fast as a beehive bids bear.

Most of us, before our child leaves the womb, are gleefully certain. We will not repeat the mistakes of our parents. *Theirs* we have catalogued. We are certain our child will be raised as well or better than were we, and our little family will *never* behave like the one we saw today at the shopping mall. Untested, certitude thrives. Predictably, the child arrives carrying with it a bookbag full of reality that, by its growing weight, smashes or at least distorts the shape of our idealism. So great an effect leaves us standing before the question of whether or not to learn. We have to decide.

Learning means flexibility and humility. It means knowing the difference between secure and sure. It means hearing beyond certitude and occasionally resigning cherished ideas because more honest or reliable ones present themselves.

It is not easy to hear communications theorist Neil Postman say in *Amusing Ourselves to Death* that our beloved "Sesame Street" is educational only in the sense that all television is educational.

> Just as reading a book—any kind of book—promotes a particular orientation toward learning, watching a television show does the same. "Little House on the Prairie," "Cheers," and "The Tonight Show" are as effective as "Sesame Street" in promoting what might be called the television style of learning. . . . "Sesame Street" does not encourage children to love school or anything about school. It encourages them to love television.

Can't anything be easy!? Not much is, really. But learning means escaping ruts. Even good ones. Our daily habits can run so deep that we no longer ride high enough to see *if* grass is growing, let alone to notice where it is greener. I do not advocate prohibiting fine television programming. I do suggest caring about careless assumptions. Learn the difference between fine things and seemingly fine things.

Enough of heavy responsibilities toward such things as faith, politics, families, and preferred programming. I quickly add that knowing when and how to take a break from seriousness is also a part of learning. Responsibilities and relationships, stress and anxiety, can be relieved by wisely closing the mind down through a bit of television, entertainment, theme parks, sillyness. Or by applying the mind to learn about trivial things or ideas, the sort that matter very little to the overall shape of things in the world but matter to us.

The habits of dabbling and diving ducks help me escape for a while the question of whether my child will finish school. Wondering about how space can curve, or why penguins do not get frostbite on their wet feet in subzero temperatures, or why frozen yogurt swirls from a spigot, just broadens my day; it solves no problems. It only helps keep me out of ruts.

Learning to put play on my calendar as well as appointments and duties is important. Learning that learning is a gift, is a gift of learning. Learning about things and ideas can fill small spaces of time or pour through a lifetime. But we must begin.

One of my favorite ways to meet new ideas I am at least minimally interested in is to check from the library a children's book on the subject. That is exactly how I learned about the power of steam and about periods of history I avoided learning about in school.

Children's books on basic astronomy enlarge my love of the sky. Adult books on this subject either overwhelm me technically or basically bore me. Children's books are usually well-written, clear, fast, and laden with more than enough information for general curiosity. A good place to start.

I mentioned earlier that questions are indispensable to listening. They are also essential to learning. What is ignorance? It is the lack of knowledge, not a lack of intelligence. Questions seek knowledge. I have a lot of questions. Friends and books are good sources for answering some of them. But a most indispensable tool for the curious is the dictionary.

Pick up the dictionary, read about a rainbow, a cell, an elephant, or an eel. What interests you? Learn about it first in the dictionary; then if it interests you more, expand your investigation. Learn about things, ideas, people. Learn your great-grandmother's maiden name, how she played as a child, her favorite dessert, her greatest childhood fear. Make an appointment with the clerk at city hall to ask some questions. How *does* a city operate? How many departments are there?

What do they do? Where do garbage trucks get washed and repaired? How much do their tires cost?

No? Not city hall? Then something, *anything,* that benefits your freedom. Ignorance is a self-imposed prison. Something always is the subject of our thinking, but the less we think about things outside ourselves the more we chain our minds to ourselves. A few people on this earth may be so utterly fascinating that they are adequate material for all their own thoughts. I just do not know any. Sorry, friends, I just do not.

Life Is Always a Lesson, Whether or Not We Learn It

I can thank my eighth-grade teacher for encouraging my love of the English language. Likely, Mrs. Bartles was responsible for placing me in advanced English my freshman year of high school. As nearly as I remember, I was a flatly average student who happened to do well in English. Fun was the driving purpose of my life. Pom-poms and off-campus passes energized my sense of purpose.

My freshman English teacher was not like me. He was an avid little theater actor and a mighty presence. He loved words, their sound, his own beautiful voice shaping them. He had us reading *Othello*. He had us discussing Shakespeare and writing papers. He had me much too busy, and I had to work very hard finding ways to circumvent this responsibility. Apparently my dedication and obvious determination to do just that paid off.

One day—fortunately I do not remember the exact circumstance or its outcome—one day, I do remember standing at the desk of my dramatic teacher and hearing him finish his (accurate) assessment of me with this phrase, "Miss Roberts, you are a dedicated gold bricker."

I did not receive this warmly—obviously I was not being complimented—but I did not blanch. I laughed a little because he did. Mostly, I stood wondering what he meant by gold bricking. Its meaning completely escaped me. Only a couple of years ago did I look up the term.

During World War II, the period of my instructor's young adulthood, a gold bricker was someone idling, or shirking duty, someone skilled at letting another do all the work. My teacher was on target. I was not into school, generally speaking. But why, for so many years, did I even remember this undefined assessment? What did it strike in me to stay with me? It struck my curiosity. It did not, as perhaps he had hoped, strike my conscience or my sense of honor. It could not. I did not know what it meant. But it struck my curiosity and lay there for years. A phrase, an opinion, stored till curiosity wanted badly enough to stop wondering and start knowing. Life is a lesson, whether or not we learn it.

My grandmother taught me one. Martha Elizabeth. She died last December, and it does not matter that she was ninety-three, that her heart was failing. I meant for Granny never to die. She is, was, an indispensable part of my life. She helped raise me, she certainly helped shape my personality, and she gave me her love of observation, of language, and of art. She was a friend.

I can hear her say, "Oh, Barbi," like no one else said it. Not that others do not address me with affection or love, it is just that no one else is Granny. One day, nearly twenty years ago, she and I were working together in my kitchen. She was visiting for a few weeks from Phoenix. It was a stressful time in my life. I was not very happy. If you had asked me then, I probably would have said that David was making me "not happy." That is how it felt, that day in my warm summer kitchen, preparing dinner with Granny, waiting for my husband to come home.

She was widowed, but I knew she had been unhappily married. Her husband was many years her senior, was never her partner, was definitely her lord. Pop had his chair, his radio, his schedule, his preferences, his daily peeled apple, and his wife to make life comfortable—for him. In striking and terrible ways, through sixty-some years, he demonstrated a lack of loyalty, a lack of love. He, of course, had his story, which makes me want to better understand. But in my kitchen, realizing Granny's tender personality and creative spirit, I wondered how she managed to survive. I wondered especially for myself. My husband was not by any stretch my grandfather, but I was suffering a long spell of being "not happy."

"Granny, didn't you ever need to count?" I asked. "How did you survive all that time in your marriage?" My grandmother leaned against the cupboard, became wistful and vulnerable, and in her gentle and resigning way said, "Oh, Barbi. You know, you just learn to die a little bit at a time." Life is a lesson.

Granny's words shot through me like twelve years of schooling compacted in a phrase. "Learn this, Barbara," the lesson said, "learn this. Do not live by dying a little bit at a time." I made a decision that late afternoon as sunshine poured through my kitchen windows, as my grandmother lightened the subject with her wonderful humor. I finished wondering; I began to learn. My personality is so like hers: I tolerate, I abide, I rarely express anger, I rarely feel it. But I knew I was finished being "just like her." I made a decision that nothing—not marriage, not future, not security, not peace—should require "dying a little at a time."

Dave and I do not have the same relationship we shared prior to that Granny lesson. The poor man was nailed the moment he came home that day. I nailed myself. We discussed the needs of our marriage; we discussed mutual responsibilities. We discussed the survival of both of us in relationship. We got better. We were not through learning, but we would never again be where we were before life offered us a chance to learn.

Whether or not we pay attention to it, all of life is a lesson. Every moment allows an assessment of the world around us and the one within us. Some lessons are momentous; others are minor. Some will hurt our feelings or our dignity; some will prove us right, delight our hearts. But nothing in life happens without eventually affecting everything else. Lessons of life are like the concentric circles left in a pond when a pebble is dropped or a leaf falls. They quietly continue whether anyone is watching or caring. Life teaches, whether or not we learn.

Conclusion

Maya Angelou, poet, educator, historian, best-selling author, actress, playwright, civil-rights activist, producer, and director, a great contemporary voice, and remarkable Renaissance woman, spoke in Tacoma, Washington. My daughter Kim and I heard her. Ms. Angelou, without a doubt, is pure talent, presence, and pleasure with a powerful punch.

She is also a woman who deserves to be angry, destroyed, defeated. In fact, for three of her childhood years she did not speak. She could not. She suffered the effects of a brutal rape. She knows "dysfunctional family" as if each letter of those two words were her breakfast, lunch, and dinner throughout childhood. They were. Ms. Angelou represents many people who have the right to be angry, to refuse to believe life has lessons worth learning, even in the midst of horror or hardship.

Rather, she is the model of a decision-maker. She decided to learn. She committed herself to survival and to a level of survival that loves, feels, risks, reaches out.

> whatever is true, . . . honorable, . . . just, . . . pure, . . . pleasing, commendable, if there is any excellence, . . . anything worthy of praise, think about these things. Keep on doing the things that you have learned.

We learn what we can endure, what it means to know ourselves and our world, how we can fail, how to survive, how to survive well. Real people are committed to shedding ignorance, to learning in order to live authentically.

CHAPTER FOUR

*L*eaning

"Straighten up!" Virtually every child hears this command applied to his posture or her behavior sometime in life. Who knows, perhaps the saying began at the Mayflower, or even before, with English Puritans who put our future aboard. Wherever it was planted it rooted, and Americans, traditionally, are loath to lean. *Leaning means to rest against or on something for support.*

I recently read about a strong, single pioneer who, like many other women of the nineteenth century, moved from east to west homesteading land. She logged trees and cut from them everything she needed, from wall logs to roof shingles. She raised livestock, hunted rabbit, frightened off bear, put down wounded or diseased animals, hauled water, planted posts, built fences, dug the outhouse pit, gathered berries, begged a garden to yield, and late by lantern light after meals mostly of corn mush, she washed out her stockings for the next day, killed crawling critters settling in her bed quilts, then crawled in herself (Molly Gloss, *Jump-Off Creek*).

Generation after generation, Americans encouraged and

practiced independence. Even church movements reflected this. Early Roman Catholic immigrants surprised the curia with new, non-European self-determination. Later, fundamental Protestantism strengthened this course by stressing a "personal" nature of salvation, individualized and privatized faith. Historically, Americans stand straight. We try not to tilt. We consider leaning a sign of weakness. But lean we must, if we are to be real.

Help? Yes. Most of us are ready *to* help others. But *to ask* for help? We are reluctant. A willingness to help others but never to ask for help ourselves is akin to a group of monkeys with one willing to groom others but who refuses reciprocation. Independence too firmly maintained signals danger. An independent primate will socially fail, then literally weaken and lose its community connection. Ditto people who fail to learn that reciprocation is a vital exchange, that leaning is strength, not a monkey on our back.

Before leaning is an action it is an attitude—one not always easily cultivated. Voices of people whose stories I have heard over the years scramble forward as examples in my mind—childhood stories of abandoning or emotionally absent parents, adult stories of broken confidences or broken promises.

What does a six-year-old know about a permanently disappearing parent? She knows absence. What does a neglected child know as well as he knows how to tie a shoe? He knows trusting, loving, depending, leaning can hurt you.

What do emotionally wounded adults learn whether or not they realize it? They learn to straighten up. Those who at some point in life leaned, only to have support jerked out from under them, long for help to come unrequested, from the outside, long for a "no risk" support. But this book is about the inside of us, about noble character. Even when we have been hurt, whether scars are old or new, we must learn again to lean, to commit ourselves to *asking for* support when we need it. Otherwise, we cease functioning well as members of community, whether our community is of friendship, organizations, marriage, or family.

Leaning risks; it declares vulnerability, it admits needing help and asks for it. It understands that independence is not always admirable, that standing up straight is not always good posture.

Jesus leaned, even from the cross. Dying, he saw two people he dearly loved—Mary, his mother, and his disciple John. Risking, leaning hard on their love for him, he entrusted them to each other. Then, as completely as any strong individual trapped in a paralyzed body must, he leaned for basic needs. He was thirsty. He said so. He, powerful and noble man that he was, leaned for relief.

The apostle Paul, independent cuss that he sometimes was, grew tender and honest when he leaned on his young friend Timothy.

Be diligent to come to me quickly . . . Get Mark and bring him with you, for he is useful to me for ministry. . . . Bring the cloak that I left . . . and the books, especially the parchments. (2 Tim. 4:9, 11, 13)

Paul is confident that the "Lord will deliver me," but he asks Timothy not to delay. "Do your utmost to come before winter." Good lean by a strong man. Leaning states a need as opposed to waiting for another to guess it, predict it, see it, or initiate aid. Sometimes real people lean just a little, sometimes a lot.

Lean a Little

Once upon a time all our family except eldest son Doug went canoeing in boundary waters between Canada and the USA. Our ten-day trek launched off from Lake #1, near Ely, Minnesota. My journal says,

Day One:

He who said, "He who rides, rows, and does not read," was right. Actually, it was David who said it, a few days before we left California, in response to my selecting books to take along. "No reading en route," he said, knowing more than I about paddling and portaging between lakes one through six.

A paddler's eyes do not consult pages, they read the horizon, the black, clear lake water, the position of the sun, and on this day, the presence of the moon. It will wax to full during our trek. Beauty binds nature's book and while there is a continuous theme, every page differs. The sun sifts light through dense shoreline growth, the wind imprints water patterns, some quite chillingly exciting. The tone is set by sounds of birds, ducks, and breeze, a paddle against water and sometimes against aluminum; sometimes aluminum in shallow water, against rocks. A human "hello" comes from rarely passing canoes, but always we hear the merciless buzzing of giant flies.

Once upon a time our family went canoeing. The next year, when a plan to repeat the ten-day trek unfurled in the minds of family men, I unfurled a memory of portaging,

The portage of all portages . . . 105 rods long (one rod = sixteen and a half feet). Do NOT visualize a smooth, straight path for our portage. This sixth portage of the day . . . came after eight hours of canoeing. Even Gordy, the wilderness lover, used the

*word "exhausted" and said "I can't take any more." But he took
a lot more.*

*We began this final path by surmounting a series of boulders,
then moved nearly straight up, foot space by foot space, between
large rocks and rigid, retired tree roots lodged between looming
trees and dense undergrowth. It wound over, down, up, around,
and finally deposited its canoe-and-supply-bearing-travelers on the
shore of Insula Lake. Three canoes reloaded, we pushed off to
find our first night's camp site.*

*For the seventh time today, we unloaded the massive amount of
gear required by our party of six. By 10:30 P.M. camp is set, all
food is strung twelve or more feet off the ground, tents are sprayed
against gathering mosquitoes, dinner and dishes are done.
Tomorrow, we row to our permanent camp.*

The next day I wrote, "How can I wake up with my hands
dirty? They were clean when I went to bed." These months
later, as conversations turned again to canoeing, I remembered
the beauty, the exciting thunderstorms, forest fomites and wild
blueberries, the sketching, reading, and writing allowed by
quiet remoteness, the delicious fish caught and eaten, conversations, campfires, family connections, the loo-loo-loo of loons,
snapping turtles, entertaining otters, mushrooms, and wild-
flowers. I remember the open-air outbox. You just could not
call it an outhouse. There was no house to it. I remembered,
too, that daughter Kim added to the margins of my camp
journal sketches of giant ants and wrote, "ants . . . about
30,000,000." She drew a massive-eyed, syringe-nosed mos-
quito, adding, "about 300,000,000." I remembered and said,
"Once upon a time is plenty for me."

"Perfect," said my quick-thinking husband. He knew this
year son Doug wanted to go but had to work. "What if . . ."
reasoned the Pine men in my absence, "what if Doug the

breakfast cook provided a reliable replacement? Then he could go!" Oh, the brilliance of these creative men! Mom cooks; she doesn't have anything important to do while we are gone. How they did reason! Actually, that is the question, how *did* they reason? How did they talk me into this harebrained exchange? How did Doug convince his employer to give it a try? How did I ever consent to such a deal? However—it happened. Doug leaned and I allowed, and then I began a week of training.

July 23, 1981

It is Thursday. This morning at 5:30 I trained to cook breakfasts and serve lunches. Last Saturday night I learned to "close." I can't believe there are so many pieces to a restaurant! Everything has to be taken apart, cleaned, emptied, and refilled. Covered, refrigerated, or shelved. Turned off, turned over, turned in, or around. There is a procedure for everything.

Today I pretty much opened the place by myself. Doug watched. Could I prep sandwiches, run the finger-hungry meat slicer, chop vegetables in the huge chopper, remember the setting numbers for tomatoes and mushrooms (#15), meats (#4), mix tuna according to the boss's recipe, make cole slaw? Can I order supplies, sack breads in freshness order, prep the salad bar and steam tables, wipe tables, straighten chairs, get trash containers, mats, signs where they belong, make quiche, prepare the cash drawer, start the grill, properly brew tea and coffee, and make lemonade? Are the serving utensils in place, the quiche utensils? The #100 serving scoops for butter and creamed cheese? Is the toaster rotating?

Are cutting trays in place, foods ready for breakfast orders? "Specials" written on morning board? Deli towels drained of their overnight soak of bleach and vinegar, rinsed in "degreaser," squeezed out, placed in appointed places around work area where foods are served? Did I read any instructions left from yesterday's night crew? Are magic markers placed in the Styrofoam cup UPSIDE DOWN? Do I remember to freshen cream pitchers, or

how to whip ten pounds of cream cheese, make dressings, reach
supplies on shelves far above my head with a long handled ladle,
how to properly supply refrigerators?

Can I properly clean the hot grill when I finish cooking,
throwing ice on it to create steam, scrape off oil and food residue,
then scrape the surface clean with a grill brick which is a black
crumbly mess, and finally perfectly wipe down all its nooks,
crannies, and knobs? Place cooling rack on top, then announce,
happily and adamantly, "the grill is closed"? Can I? Remember,
it is worth it, I pull in three dollars and thirty-five cents an hour.

I leaned hard on Doug in that week of training. My inadequacies beamed. I desperately needed help. I learned to lean hard on Charlie, the dishwasher whose expansive English vocabulary ran from, "Oh, yeah? Good morning. Here. It's okay. I don't comprehendo" to "I won't be in today; I'm sick," which he learned to say over the phone on Fridays. Charlie stayed busy busting boxes down, sweeping the patio eating area, rolling pie crusts for the pastry chef, slicing fruit for lunch setup, and reaching for me those heavy containers high over my head. I did not mind doing dishes for him on Fridays.

In fact, I did not mind any of the work I did, once I learned to flip the eggs back into the pan rather than onto the floor and to handle four or five orders at a time. Once the rhythm of my duties regulated, I was whistling. But in training, I leaned hard on Doug. Leaning a little can involve leaning hard for a little time or leaning light for a long time. But a little lean never means leaning long and hard—that defines "to lean a lot." Doug and I reciprocated with little leans.

Shortly after my husband and sons left for Minnesota boundary waters and I was expertly opening for business at 6:30 A.M., I had reason to lean a little on some friends. The cause of it came in on Thursday of my first week at work. A man ordered coffee. Not "any" man but one who frightened me. He came early, stayed late. He did not speak, he was not social, but he stayed. He watched. He watched me work. He stayed nearly two hours in our small space, with his long blue-jeaned legs, dark leather jacket, wide leather spiked wristband, cowboy hat, narrowed eyes, and silence. I rejoiced when the place crowded, hoping the crowd would filter his gaze and my growing discomfort. I worked hard in my mind trying to "straighten up."

He was back Friday morning. And Monday, as we opened. By gesture, grunts, and occasional word, he ordered coffee, got refills, and sat. Watching. By Tuesday it occurred to me that if this man proved dangerous, the petite pastry chef and I were trapped. The door he came through, and near which he sat, was our only door. Who would hear us at 6:30 A.M. if we screamed? I looked at the chef's knives hanging in the narrow kitchen and worried. By the middle of my second week of work I wrote, "I was honestly so frightened by his 6:30 A.M. arrival that my heart sped up, my head created enormous pressure at the forehead and temples, and I seriously considered locking myself in the bathroom till he left."

Perhaps he was harmless, even a nice guy. Perhaps I was exaggerating fear. This must be what it means to be neurotic, I thought. Neurotic or not, I leaned a little. I told the manager of my concern. He found my fear exaggerated (read neurotic). "He's a little strange, but he's never bothered anyone." Leaning is not always rewarded. Managers solve problems, and mine did by suggesting I call him at home if I had trouble. "I just live ten minutes away." Gee, why didn't I feel comforted?

I needed support, but not even the amazing baker, who entered the restaurant alone two hours before me, considered my fear legitimate. "Too sensitive," she said, growling out of her small body a huge Italian impatience with my fear. She was tough and fearless, this woman who grew up with nearly a dozen brothers. I suppose I looked foolish, sounded odd, but I needed help. I leaned a new direction.

I called friends from our church who kindly arranged to eat breakfast out, early. Yes it inconvenienced them. Leaning does. That is why we are so apt to avoid doing it. My friend Linda arrived with her three teenagers for a week's visit from Colorado. "Blessed are the teenagers who rise early on a summer day, for they shall receive a large breakfast." Kids—hers, mine, and friends of my daughter—came to eat, early. I refused to "straighten up" or be alone in this small place. My journal says "I am thoroughly spooked. I dread work. But . . . I go." That is, I *was* going. On time. Until Thursday of my second week. Instead of my usual departure at 5:30 A.M., I was sleeping.

> *UNBELIEVABLE! I overslept! At ten till six I woke up. I quickly call the restaurant to say I am on my way. Linda is madly rushing through the house, waking people to go with us.*
>
> *"Alena? This is Barb. I overslept but I will be there in a minute."*
>
> *"Oh, Ba-baa-ra," said an obviously terrified Alena in her gravelly voice. "You know that man?"*
>
> *"The tall one?"*
>
> *"Yeah, with the cowboy hat. He's here! He's right outside, and I'm so scared!"*
>
> *"Oh, Alena! LINDA!" I yell. "That guy is there!" Lin, who owned and managed a restaurant, and knew herself capable of taking over, forbids my going. She rounds up kids. Alena continued,*
>
> *"And, I don't got the door locked. I think you are coming so I left the door unlocked. Can you do something? Hurry, please."*

"My friends are coming now. They'll be there within five minutes. Just stay in the kitchen."

"Oh, I'm so scared." She had her eye on the chef's knives, she said. In case.

Can you believe it? He was there. Outside the restaurant door at 5:30 A.M. Had I gotten to work on time and walked up to that place . . . I cannot bear the thought of my fear.

Linda and five teenagers converge on the restaurant, entering as the "tall man" asks for coffee. At home, I decide to call the police.

I explain the situation to a dispatcher—a woman employee alone in a restaurant with the door unlocked and a "scary sort of man at the front door."

"What is the man doing?" asked the cool dispatcher.

"He's doing nothing. We don't want him to do anything. I just wonder if you could ask a policeman to casually go there 'for coffee'? Just to keep an eye on the situation till my friends arrive?" She reluctantly offers "to see."

Linda calls, "We're here," she whispers. "Get your manager here fast. This guy is strange. And don't you dare come here till I call and tell you he is gone."

Now . . . add to the morning's excitement three police cars, lights flashing, six policemen approaching the building, slowly moving up to it and finally, ah, casually, bursting in with this forceful announcement: "We've had a call of disturbance at this location. Is there a problem?"

Oh, right. Everyone stood stunned. Everyone.

Police leave without coffee. My manager arrived about an hour later, just minutes after the tall man left. I arrived five minutes after that.

Linda managed what I had not. She convinced my boss to have a man on hand for morning openings. Apparently even barging police did us a service. The man did not return again, at least not during my breakfast shift tenure. I earned a little paycheck. Doug enjoyed a glorious time in Minnesota. He resumed his kitchen and the drama closed. Most leaning does end without deserving headlines, without total exhaustion.

All leaning requires a question, then action. First, "Is this something I can and should do on my own?" If so, personal responsibility rises to the fore, and no lean is merited. If not, then act. Ask for help. Theologically speaking, these are the right responses to any paraenesis. That is, any biblical passage that commands personal behavior benefiting the Christian community at large and that morally and ethically reflects in us what God has redemptively done *for* us.

About the only drawback to leaning a little is the risk of embarrassment, appearing less than perfectly capable or independent. A little lean usually involves an adjustment of pride or of self-image and requires short spurts of time or effort from others. Or a long run of light support.

Little leans occur often and seldom draw attention. But to lean a lot? To lean a lot means to swallow pride, to admit genuine worry or concern, to deeply involve people, perhaps even tax them, to depart from a normal course, to unavoidably attract some attention. I learned a lot about leaning a lot from the Gregg family.

Lean a Lot

What a year or two this family recently involved me in. First, our friend Cal Gregg was dying of cancer. "I know you walked through this with Linda," he said to me one day over coffee. "Will you do it for me?" I felt a great kinship to long-ago Nehemiah who, when confronted with a hard question from King Artaxerxes, became "dreadfully afraid" so he "prayed to the God of heaven." Dreadfully afraid, we began that very day.

Then, his incredibly talented and bright sixteen-year-old son Chris began meeting with me regularly so he could talk and figure. Over the phone, over pizza and soft drinks, or hot tea and popcorn, he challenged my brain and spirit. "If you must hurt, hurt well," he heard me say once and decided he wanted to do that. We worked together on how to hurt.

Nearly daily by phone or visit, I caught up with his mom, my friend and neighbor Nancy. Nancy's parents were on an extended visit from Ohio, and her father, too, was undergoing chemotherapy treatments. That the Gregg family hurt is an understatement. But never does only one thing go on at a time. There was more than hurt at their house. Great joy was brewing around their eldest son, Roger, a familiar figure to me since he and our son Gordy were high school buddies. Now, fairly well recovered from an unchosen divorce, he was dating everyone's favorite person, Gloria, a twenty-nine-year-old beauty with a great love for the Dodgers baseball team and an exuberant involvement with high schoolers in her church.

How nice for me that Gloria and I frequently met together before Roger entered the picture. Our fortnightly occasions quickly became "smile all night" sessions where she evaluated and celebrated falling irretrievably in love. But, not the half was known—to anyone. Forgive the pun; it was a lean year for the Gregg family.

In late summer Roger and Gloria became pregnant. They leaned; I supported. For well-founded reasons but not perfect ones, we agreed that since they were nearly thirty years old not seventeen, since pregnancy was a fact and there was no plan to change that, since they needed to confirm their commitment to one another and not only to a pregnancy, since they anticipated some flak once the news was out, they needed some time. They wanted to settle their own issues before dealing with responses of family and community. I urged them to be courageous enough to chart their own course, to marry and tell when the time was right for them, not "because of" and not for people who count on their fingers the months before a child is born. Darned if they didn't take me seriously. I was beginning to fidget as they delayed, as seasons shifted.

Near November's end, Roger visited his father, Cal, and observed the absence of familiar humor and hope. Cal was depressed, weary with pain, suffering effects of chemotherapy, willing to die. Roger knew he held a powerful distraction. "Dad, you have to keep living. Gloria and I are getting married soon, and you are going to be a grandfather. If the baby is a boy, we plan to name him after you." A grandchild! His first. Cal had new incentive to live, to fight cancer. And fight he did. This country-western music lover started humming the "Gloria" at the oddest times and wore his son's secret as a perpetual grin.

No one had a wit quite as quick as Cal's. One near-Christmas day I dropped by their business to see Nancy. Cal was there and "knew I knew." He signaled me aside and after a brief greeting said with gentle irreverence, "You know, I remember another special woman who got pregnant before she was married, and it worked out really well that time. I think it will this time, too."

Well, it did. They waited to be married longer than any of us would recommend. I mean *wait*. But in December they married in deep, committed love. The brouhaha it caused, a powerful one and not without some justification, blew over for the most part by April when their beautiful son was born and named for his paternal grandfather. Cal lived till June, long enough to go bananas over his grandchild, to pour love and blessing on his new, radiant daughter-in-law, and to be comforted in dying by cradling a child bearing his name.

One thing the independent, self-sufficient, private Greggs had to learn in that very hard period of small scandal and large disease was to swallow pride and lean, a lot. Cal was best at it. I was proud of his allowing friends to learn with him about dying, to assist him in it. Roger and Gloria caught baskets full of criticism. I, too, for my manner of supporting them. But they leaned a lot and astounded me by their composure. Some people were saddened or angered by the loss of Gloria as an ideal model of a Christian single woman. That Roger was her first sexual partner, that she did not abort a baby, received less attention than the fact that when she chose to be sexually involved, she did not immediately resign from working with high school kids. If my counsel or her concern were perfect, she surely would have; it would have saved much grief. But she and Roger did a good job of leaning in a gale of criticism. They had a complicated start, what with grieving Cal, disappointing some family members, shocking people generally, and settling into marriage and parenthood.

Chris worked to understand criticisms lodged against his brother. He struggled with reactions of his peers toward him as he privately absorbed the pain of his father's illness. He worked hard to shoulder the effects of loss. Chris just was not always himself. Buddies wanted him to focus on baseball, and good grades, and girls, as he usually did, but now reality was basically bad news. One sweet friend, Kathy, walked especially close. Some worked hard to understand Chris, and Chris worked hard to understand others. All in all, he has grieved well what we all wish never occurred.

But Nancy? My dear friend Nancy is likely to give away the bulb out of her only lamp, lend directions and a siphon hose to a car thief, and publish her cherished, secret recipe. Nancy habitually gives. She prefers not to lean, ever. In the beginning of Cal's crisis, she behaved like an independent primate. In fact, she increasingly tended others but refused to accept tending to the point that people wondered if she understood the situation. In truth, she was so aware, so terrified, so unaccustomed to needing support, that she retreated. Nancy was a well-constructed braided rug unraveling. Eventually, she was forced to repair or ruin. She opted for repair.

In learning to lean a lot she allowed three important things. First, she allowed her friend Sue to organize a broad group of people to assist her: driving her father and husband to doctors appointments, running errands, ironing, preparing a few meals, visiting, assisting Cal when he was finally forced home for good, generally covering chores impossible for Nancy, who now assumed full responsibility of a small family business. F.O.G. was formed: Friends of Greggs.

She allowed Hospice to enter the picture. Hospice counseled, taught the family how to set up and prepare for Cal's dying at home, supplied nursing visits at the necessary time. Then, on a more intimate level, Cal and Nancy allowed the development of the "Grapple Group." We really meant to find a better name, we seven couples that met. We meant to grapple with some hard experiences under a better name, but we never found one. So, for well over a year, we met every other week, studying Scripture, praying, supporting, sharing communion, meals, and deliberate community. We sponsored a laugh night for Cal, learned to talk about unspeakable subjects, learned to commit ourselves to one another, learned that while the Greggs were our primary concern, every one of us needed help. We learned to keep laughing, hoping, caring while we cried together. We learned to assume tasks that the Greggs could no longer personally tend, to prepare well for an unacceptable eventuality. The Gregg lean grew great, and the Grapple Group was strong enough to let it lean a lot.

The *requirement* for leaning is a change of posture—attitudinal posture. No more pride about standing up straight. No more hyper-independence, no more isolation within a group meant to be healthy by reciprocation. Emotional health requires a tilt, like walking in a strong wind. The *wisdom* of leaning lies in learning how much support you need in order to stay on your feet. Leaning and its affects on others can vary as greatly as the slaps of an ocean against the shore. Effective barriers range from reef grasses or short concrete walls to massive stacks of boulders or deeply driven pilings, depending upon the level of force that strikes. Leaning a lot, wisely, means acknowledging great need, yes. It also means not asking reef grass to do the holding work of boulders, not calling for boulders when a small wall will do. A lot of leaning requires a lot of vulnerability and usually more than one person to catch the force of crashing reality. Cal was instantly ready. Nancy learned to lean . . . a lot.

When a Lean Isn't

A cry for help that rejects reciprocation describes not leaning but using. Sometimes we who assist fail to notice our being used and consequently do not help wisely. In a hot midsummer of our children's teen years, I returned from traveling to meet a sixteen-year-old boy our son invited to live with us. Doug, recently graduated from high school and kicking up his own moral storm, gathered that this boy needed help and knew we had some at our house. I will call him Monte. We met around the dining room table where so many decisions of our family are made, agreed to, challenged, or ignored. We tried to explain our family, and he tried to explain himself. My journal says, "There has been trauma, lying, drinking, pot, prescription drug abuse, irresponsibility, fighting, etc. Will we be able to help?"

I do not know if we did. But I do know that by the time our son Gordy came home from two weeks of camp to find Monte sharing his room, my journal already recorded drinking bouts, a few fights, and a list of Monte's injuries: a tooth is chipped, a swollen lip, elbow stitches, bruised cheek and head.

I knew that Gordy was good for Monte when I overheard their first private conversation. Gordy said, "Is that your Snoopy dog?" pointing to a small stuffed dog on Monte's pillow. "Do you sleep with it?"

"Ah, well, yeah," came a cautious reply.

"Oh. I've got a blanket around here somewhere. My mom made it when I was born. I call it Trusty."

Tensions melted. Compatible relationships began. Monte slipped comfortably into the line of sulking siblings arguing before school over the one bathroom they shared. We thought Monte was leaning on our family. Maybe even he hoped he was, but he was not. He did not lean; he could not. He used. Had we met him six months earlier than we did, we would have met a good kid unconsciously and adoringly linked to his older brother, earning above-average grades, expressing a great sense of humor, a love of surfing, a busy social life. Then, strike one, strike two. His older brother died and nearly simultaneously his parents divorced. Suddenly, twice stunned, Monte worked at straightening up, way up. He did not lean, he handled loss with his fists, drugs, and anger. My journal says,

Monte comes home late Wednesday night . . . At about 9:30 P.M. he confronts me. "You've taken my things."

"I took your knife and club. True."

"I want them now," he replied.

"No."

The verbal push begins again. He needs to defend himself, he says. He only wants them in his room. Do I want him to get killed? he asks. I assure him there are alternatives to fights. He is not interested in alternatives.

We argued loudly about the removal of weapons. "My dad lets me have them," he tells me. "Then, I will give them to your dad and he can give them to you if he chooses, but you cannot live here with weapons."

Two months later I wrote,

Monday. First day of school

Hot. Very hot. Kim is excited, Gordy is edgy, Monte is in a fight and suspended for a day and a half. We begin again. "But everybody knows its not my fault," he says happily.

Tuesday

Monte is at home. He cleans blinds for me. We discuss the ramifications of the fight. He sees retaliation as an essential response.

Today his father was hospitalized and even though it is not threatening, Monte goes crazy with fear. They fight, they cannot live together, but he surely cannot live without him. He visits his dad in the hospital, goes for a beer afterward, and then home to bed, crying. High, I think. Dangerously agitated. I go to him to see if he needs to talk.

"I gotta hit something. Man, I gotta hit something."

"Don't hit me," I ask.

"No, but I gotta hit something. My dad brought me a mattress once. I hav'ta hit something hard."

So, I brought in a couch cushion. He slugs with violence in language and physical force. He is teetering on hysteria.

"Gotta walk. Cotton-mouth." Dave and Doug wake up, try to help. Gordy is away, Kim sleeps through it all. Again and again he repeats, "gotta walk," staggers, trips over a fan set on the floor, runs his fingers through his hair.

Doug, Dave, and I are frightened, thinking of the next step. Doug says, "Let's go run." Out the door they go. Both in boxer shorts, neither thinking about it. Did Monte have on any shoes? I don't think so. They run around the rural blocks and return when Monte is finally able to walk down the drive. To bed.

I called the mental health team for advice while the guys ran. Dave is calm, my stomach is twisted, sick. Tomorrow I have a full schedule. Who cares? Another day with Monte passes. Will they ever end?

Wednesday

Dark days for me . . . Monte gets the best of me. His hyper behavior is exhausting. His high opinion of himself, exasperating. He is home from school with a tale of a "nearly in a fight." He loves it. Thrives on excess and excitement.

I am tired. Monte, Monte. Will he ever yield? Will we ever be able to open his heart to good? What will it take?

Thursday we confronted him. His school counselor said he was not attending class. We gave him a choice. By Saturday afternoon, he had to choose to change his pattern and stay with us or declare his satisfaction with how things were and leave. Some cooperation had to occur. I asked Monte to mentally stand across the room and observe himself. "Tell me about him," I said.

"He likes to get drunk, likes drugs, likes to talk to girls, likes to fight."

"Is that good?" I asked.

"No, but it's fun."

That journal page ends with this sentence: "Change is not wanted but a house is." Monte wanted to stay, of course. He wanted to use. He did not lean; he needed no rest, no support. He needed only a place.

October. Monday
David's birthday.
So difficult to communicate sense to Monte. He will risk all for his independence.
"Do you know we care for you, Monte?"
"You just said you do."
"But do you know?"
He repeats what he had just said.
"Do you believe us? That we care?"
Quietly, "I guess."
We ask for one week of cooperation with basic family rules. Goodness knows, we have few. No. He sees any rule as a prison. "Wants out."
Within thirty minutes he leaves us. Ouch, says my heart.

In the summer of the second canoe trip, while I fretted over a tall man wearing a cowboy hat, Monte reappeared. Two years had passed since we saw him last, and with those years a felony, some jail time, total estrangement from his family but nary a hair less charm. Along with Linda and her crew of kids, he spent a few days in our home. He was among those who came into the restaurant early to eat, to loan me a sense of safety. He had a vague story or two about his present situation, but he appeared sober (read appeared). I was genuinely glad to see him; we all love him.

Men of our church provided him with work he needed. Sensing the odds but ignoring the reality, I gave Monte my little paycheck from the restaurant to help pay for a technical school course. Naturally, I should have mailed my check to the school. Hindsight = 20/20. It was to Monte's great disadvantage that our family lacked discernment about the difference between leaning and using. He desperately needed someone with bold, street-smart awareness to confront his manipulative skills.

My urging Monte to noble character when his own was so wounded was akin to urging a three-legged dog to walk on all fours. They both suffer more from "cannot" than "will not." But Monte left, the Pine men returned from canoeing, and Linda's clan returned to Colorado. Monte was arrested a couple of days later, then called after a few days in jail.

"Hello, Mom" came his resilient voice. "I'm leaving in five minutes. Your check is in my hand; it's not going for anything but school." Often users, like dieters, sincerely mean to do well. Who knows the real line or the real struggle between "cannot" and "will not." A summer or so later, a "born-again" Monte called from a distant state. Monte who, yes, had cashed my check but never reached school. He was in drug rehabilitation, he said. We hope so. We have not heard again.

In a San Francisco art exhibit, hanging beside a landscape painting done by Pissarro in 1876, I read this critic's comment. "Seen up close [Pissarro's landscapes] are incomprehensible and hideous; seen from a distance they are hideous and incomprehensible." Whether the art critic was correct matters little to me. I am not a great Pissarro fan. Only, the comment expresses how I feel about "using." No matter how you look at it, no matter the patience you apply to it, you can turn it in any light, at any angle, and you will always see the same thing—complete self concern. Using is hideous and incomprehensible, not because the deeds involved are necessarily evil but because they are completely self-serving. For whatever reasons, users require and request but do not restore or reciprocate.

Conclusion

Leaners are people who trust that the healthiest state of individualism is individualism within community. They know that reciprocation is not an emergency behavior but an excellent one. That a slight tilt produces rest, not exploitation. Jack Smith wrote in the *L. A. Times* about a flight attendant who served a great American boxing champion aboard her flight.

"Please fasten your seatbelt," she said, noticing he had not.

"Superman don't need no seatbelt," he replied.

"Superman don't need no airplane," she responded in a flash. That is the truth in a nutshell. Superman don't need nothin' but a phone booth. But unless we are above the human situation, we will at times need to lean. Rigid independence deserves no bouquets.

> I say to everyone among you not to think of yourself more highly than you ought to think, but to think with sober judgment . . . we are members of one another . . . Live in harmony with one another; do not be haughty, . . . do not claim to be wiser than you are.

So says the New Testament in the twelfth chapter (vv. 3, 5, 16 NRSV) of Romans. The passage encourages community by discouraging unrealistic individualism. Real people must face up to needs and limitations. They swallow pride and allow others to support. Straighten up? Not always.

CHAPTER FIVE

*L*oaning

When your heart is involved, listening evokes quite a different response than when you hear general conversation. I am remembering a particular week during which I listened to a woman, a victim of childhood incest and now hospitalized, recovering from rape; to my grandmother, losing her independence and, with it, her great love of life; to my fifty-two-year-old friend, Cal, dying but not wanting to; to my twenty-five-year-old daughter announcing her engagement; to a friend's sorrow over the death of her beloved old dog; to my geneticist friend, patiently guiding me through functions of the brain.

I listened to them, but I do not have their experiences, I cannot be them. Still, when I hear what they say, I can *loan* my whole self to them. I bounced on the bed with my happy daughter. I sat on the floor and cried with my dying friend. I can say, "Arggg . . . my head is full!" to my geneticist friend and thank him for sharing his brilliance. I can pay attention and loan myself to other people's lives.

Surely few people are so bitterly wounded that they cannot appreciate a gesture of kindness,

an offer of help,
a compliment, encouragement,
a cup of coffee together,
an inquiry about their life,
cookies shared, a movie, a note, an errand run,
a house cleaned, meal cooked, auto repaired,
a loan of yourself.

It is not always fun or convenient to loan ourselves to others, *to be deliberately and voluntarily involved*. It gets in the way of our plans and eats our energy. It can be a big bother. But, it *is* noble. That is, true loaning is. Surrendering to obligations or to guilt-induced assistance, or fulfilling some duty requires no nobility.

"I have to go help my sister hang draperies." Fine. "I have to" is obligation; it is not loaning. Obligations often, and rightfully, need filling. The turning lane between obligation and loan is only one decision wide: the decision to give yourself voluntarily, no strings attached, to a person who can benefit from your contribution, whether for months or minutes, whether deserved or not.

I once spent some minutes that seemed like a month. A woman invited me out for lunch (it was delicious). She wanted me to hear her problem. I loaned myself. Sitting on a patio, overlooking a city, eating wonderful food on a beautiful day, I listened to her confess her dislike of me. She was jealous, she said frankly between bites and smiles. I represented things she wanted for herself and somehow this offended her. She did not need to change; she only needed me to know. Believe me, I knew.

I went home, my head spinning with the perplexing experience. I called her and asked something like, "Have I done something specifically for which I should apologize?" No, she assured me, it was her problem. It helped her to be able to say it to me, that's all.

Well, how nice to be able to help people. I pray such opportunities will rarely arise. But I can tell you, because *loaning is a choice and not an obligation,* since my responsibility in this situation was *to her* not *for her,* I began shedding frustration even as my lunch digested. I was stunned but not cheated. Loaning is involvement, but it is not demand; it is cooperation, but it is not adhesion; it is hope but not expectation; it is giving yourself but with no guarantees that you wind up a hero or come home with a prize. Loaning comes from the heart, but it has to be hard-nosed sensible. It never goes "after something"; it always gives something. It gives *you,* for a time, with no promise of reward. That, no doubt, is why it must be deliberate.

Then, *loaning is not conditional.* My husband once struck upon an idea to answer to the transportation problem of a teenage friend while at the same time reducing the inventory of our garage (that garage is *his*). There in the tumble of things stood a bright red moped, unused, gathering cobwebs, a remnant from the fuel crunch and days when we rode around town with helmets on our heads. Dave was pleased to give it away. That was good and kind.

"But if he takes it, he has to wear a helmet, he cannot let other kids drive it, no riding double, he must get the brake handle fixed, he—" said David, being his usual sensible self.

"You can't do that," I argued. You can urge, you can recommend, you can talk to his parents and see what their rules will be before you decide to give, but you cannot set the rules for them. You cannot control how a gift is used, only whether the gift will be given. Dave wanted to loan and control outcome. He pinned conditions on the wrong piece of the plan. Loaning cannot do that. Loaning steps into the situation of others and assists them, there. Or for good reasons we choose not to step in at all. Of course, there are situations where we *can* call the shots, where we help make the rules, but, in loaning, we do not go forward with "conditions" pinned to our pockets. Dave admirably controlled himself and gave away the moped.

Clearly, loaning is not as common as one might hope. Spontaneous involvement is common, duty is, even conditional help is, but loaning is not. And, I think, for at least these three reasons.

Why Not?

First, we are frequently convinced that people need to "deserve" our assistance.

"Will you help me with this?"

"Why should I?" comes a response which implies the need of a good reason. *"Should" implies a conditional situation. If* a person deserves my presence, if I support their efforts, if I get something out of it . . . *then* I reward them.

Quite to the contrary, a person loans because that is what goodness does. It is the nature of kindness; it is the offspring of largesse and maturity.

"Why should I?" The answer is not because a person's cause or purpose earns my aid but because something inside me responds to need. Because noble attitudes lend without owning, because we follow the formula for healthy relationships found in the twelfth chapter of the Epistle to Romans: "in honor [give] preference to one another; not lagging in diligence" (vv. 10–11).

Why does a cat purr? Sorry, but not because of circumstance. It is a cat's nature to purr. Circumstance can encourage purring, but circumstance does not a purr create. Hopefully, those occasions when we truly "should not" loan ourselves to another emerge from wise deliberation or for appropriate reasons rather than from our own disappointed or unmet expectations.

I am now old enough to start reading about hormone replacement therapy and to love solitude. In my late twenties and early thirties, my life was public, my time away from family filled with encouraging faith in others. I loved Scripture, I loved the Lord, I was deeply involved in teaching Bible. No one could have been more surprised than I, then, when a conflict slumbering in a distant corner of my soul came begging attention.

When I was a child, nearly every person I knew well was a declaring Christian. Everyone, that is, but my much adored father. I was a spiritually sensitive child, and, in light of my training, I worried about his eternal fate. My heart panicked in the night with thoughts that my daddy could die and go to hell. And panic finally moved me one night to the side of his bed where I woke him and begged him to tell me if he *was saved*.

"I'm a Christian, Punkie, but not like you are," he said. Returning to my room, I tried to figure. With little notice, as I grew so also grew a discomfort with much of what I received doctrinally, with unbecoming but familiar practices among my fellow Christians, and the paradox of my "outsider" father's unchurched but clearly admirable—can I say Christlike—life.

Now, as an adult and uninvited, that child's crisis festered. It prompted a refitting of my faith. It was as if childhood training needed cutting away, like the shirt of a shooting victim. A mind needed healing, a properly-sized adult faith needed tailoring. It took three years. I wrote a poem during that crisis, at the point of feeling weak and spiritually naked. It sprang from Psalm 34:18,

> Have you ever been a Christian
> When you weren't in love with God?
> When phrases "Praise the Lord" and
> "Thank you, Jesus,"
> Grate like sand well hid in lettuce?
>
> Have you ever felt
> That smiling members of the body
> Whose lamps are lit, not hid under meal-tubs,
> Gather as a Sunday flame
> Coruscating inner crannies
> Where stands your well-cloaked darkness?
>
> A few, just a few,
> See your lamp's not lit
> Shade their own
> To spare your tired eyes
> And quietly lend oil.

A few lend oil. Many cannot in this sort of situation. Failing faith frightens many saints. But a few lend oil. Not because they "should," not because I earned it, not because they are guaranteed success. One such friend is Chris. The poem honors her. She is radically Christian. She loves God and His people but neither unrealistically. Chris saw my lamp was not lit. She knew I could barely tolerate bright, beaming Christians.

She quietly loaned herself and allowed her faith to carry me along for as long as it would take me to walk again in my own.

Shortly after that painful season I attended a writer's workshop. The poem you just read was critiqued by a published poet serving on faculty. Several of us sat with him around a table while he read our work. A few pieces of mine had earned his approval, so I felt unthreatened as he picked up this poem. He began to read, then stopped, put it down, saying, "Who wrote this?" I gathered from his tone to expect no admiration. "I did," I admitted.

"Rewrite it," he ordered. "You can't be a Christian and not love God."

"No?" I thought. "I am a Christian, and I guarantee you when I wrote that, I was not in love with God," I said.

No wonder so many spiritual struggles are private, quiet struggles. Mine was. A few friends knew. A few lent oil, lent themselves. That is all it takes. Encouragement, wisdom, presence, listening, yes. Shoulds, should nots, demands or expectations, no. Just a deliberate giving of unearned shoulders and support.

Second, loaning can be deterred by a fear of losing control. True, when we loan ourselves, a certain amount of circumstantial control is lost. When we contribute to the needs of others, we do things, go places, taste foods, read books, hear conversations, clean houses, repair fences, cry, laugh, stay out, drop in, calm down, and shut up, for their sake. We hear in order to listen, we may very well influence, but we do not loan ourselves demanding that. We do lose a certain amount of control when we loan ourselves.

My mother replaced a good couch with a better one. Neither my brother nor I needed the first one, but we know a young woman who manages to squeeze from little income a remarkable existence for herself and her children. "She might like to have it," I suggested.

A few telephone calls later I asked Mom about it. "Well, I'd like to give it to her," she said, "but you know her kids are going to jump on it and ruin it."

I laughed and laughed. "Good, Mom, give it to Salvation Army. You'll have a lot more control over how it is treated, right?" So people jump on things we give. Imagine the joy giving brings in the meantime. How often do we get the opportunity to drop a heavy expanse of happiness into someone's living room, literally. Mom was having a hard time loaning out of abundance because she worried about how her gift would be treated. She is a fine woman. I think it will not take long for her to overcome her need to control.

Have you ever tried to give something to someone without actually letting go of it? Ever experience those embarrassing seconds in an exchange when no one is sure who should release or grasp first? Gotta let go to let go. Advising doesn't, teaching doesn't, tutoring doesn't, even assisting doesn't always, but loaning means letting go.

Third, we hesitate loaning ourselves to others because we fear it somehow diminishes our freedom. That it does. How very perceptive of us. Perhaps nothing demonstrates more clearly why commitment rather than surrender must govern the dailyness of our lives. So many things to do, so many people to do them with or for. Either we make deliberate choices about our time and activities or we succumb to a circuit of demands like a roller coaster rider released at the highest point of the track. Forget steering—all you do is hold on and hope the car does. You may feel free, what with all that frantic busyness blowing your hair straight out, but you are not free. You are going where forces whip you. Loaning does diminish freedom, but only to the extent we allow. It also diminishes frenzy, self-centeredness, anger, pettiness, frustration, and regret.

In the fall of 1991, at Yosemite National Park, Mark Wellman and Mike Corbett scaled Half Dome. For two weeks they inched their way along the mountain's sheer cliff as spectators watched from some 2,000 feet below. A newspaper article I read about this particular climb said there was great concern for the physical well-being of Mike Corbett, "Yosemite's most experienced rock climber." He suffered numbness in his arms. "With Corbett leading, they had to inch up the final 75 feet of 2,200 foot Half Dome's vertical face to reach the summit. Part of the climb required them to swing out on their rope eight to ten feet from the wall to get above an overhang."

That might not seem like much to experienced climbers, but now the rest of the story. Mark Wellman is a paraplegic. This climbing enthusiast requires help. Enter Mike Corbett. Enter loaning. Corbett's job was doubled. No wonder his arms tired, got numb. Basically, he climbed the mountain twice. First, he climbed and set pitons, then after Mark pulled himself up, hand over hand, Mike returned to the original position to clean up the equipment. He then climbed past Mark, set the next increment, moved back down, removed equipment, climbed. . . .

Exhausted, in danger of dehydration, impeded by the mountain for days longer than expected, these two made history. With the loan of the best climber around, Mark Wellman made the first major rock climb by a paraplegic. Did Mike Corbett give up some freedom? He did. For nearly two weeks he climbed at another man's pace, in another man's style. He did twice the work. He exhausted himself. He deliberately gave up freedom; he voluntarily knocked himself out. "Why should

I?" was answered by noble character. True, you betcha; loaning diminishes personal freedom. But, oh, what a beautiful cutback.

What Could Be Worse?

In the early days of the Boeing 707, I followed my lieutenant husband to the island of Okinawa. You may remember my listening lesson that occurred there. You do not know that while my mother and father, most of my uncles, my brother, my husband, his brother, and my father-in-law were all pilots, I was terrified of flying. Put a capital *T* on terrified. In January of 1960, my dog Taco and I started the serious job of moving halfway around the world—through the air. The dog jetted on the relatively new 707. I went on a four-engine prop job. I did not regularly keep a journal then, but I did write this, probably thinking it would be the last thing I ever wrote:

> *Flight C827 to Okinawa on a chartered Flying Tigers DC7 from Travis AFB was delayed three and a half hours but finally raised its gear at 11:40 P.M., January 10th. My parents soothe my fears by phone, assuring me non-scheduled airlines can be safe.*
>
> *Nine hours to Honolulu, two hours wait. Seven hours to Wake Island; one hour stop over. What a tiny, humid place! Gooney birds! Ten hours to Okinawa arriving January 13th at 11:45 P.M. island time and date. Dave was waiting at the ramp for me.*

Twenty-six hours, two dulled ears, and two fuel stops later, I arrived in Okinawa. Tired, but alive. It helped considerably that my mother outfitted me for the trip. Thanks to her travel wisdom I had comfortable slacks to change into once en route.

I had writing materials, a familiar Bible, fellow travelers who taught me to play gin rummy, and a hardback copy of Michener's book, *Hawaii*. *Hawaii* was a gift from my mother's dearest friend, Agnes. Needless to say, time permitted my reading well into it. I loved it. And once I settled in Okinawa and finished it, I loaned it to fellow Air Force wives. The last woman I loaned it to managed never to return it. Months passed and my many requests for it passed with them. My book, new, jacketed, and lovingly inscribed, seemed hopelessly gone. Months more passed, in fact, years. We were now parents of two little boys conceived and born on Okinawa. We were packing for our return to the States when I begged a final time for the return of my book (attached as I am to certain books). I urged the borrower to track it down. It was not a new book I wanted; I wanted my book.

One afternoon I returned home from errands and at my front step was a bag holding my book. Joy of joys! It was tattered, and without its jacket, but there it was, *Hawaii,* by Michener. Yes! Then, I opened it. The inscription said,

> To Wayne and Barbara,
> from Dorothy Hix
> Christmas, 1959

To say the least, I was mystified. This was the right title but the wrong book. I called the borrower, hoping to clear up the mistake. It was remarkable that the inscription was to a Barbara, but there was no Wayne in my life and I still have no idea who Dorothy Hix is.

I was told huffily that it was the book she borrowed from me. She returned my book and that was that. That *was* that. I still have that jacketless, orphaned book on my shelf. I still resent the fact that my book, with the expression of love from Agnes, is somewhere else and this book is not mine. The problem? I loaned one thing and got back another.

What could be worse than to loan ourselves, not a book, only to learn that through neglect, power, audacity, cunning, charm, goodness, selfishness, nobility, or persuasion, a borrower has influenced us, affected us, even changed us. What could be worse? Never changing, that is what. Never being influenced, never being affected, never being challenged, that is what could be worse.

When we loan ourselves, we run the risk of others affecting us. I know my behavior in the following story may prompt disapproval in some readers. I do not tell the story to be affirmed or corrected. I ask, as Charles Kuralt sometimes does on the "Sunday Morning" show, "If you write me, please do not write me about this."

The Story

Shortly after America's bicentennial celebration, a barely sixteen-year-old Maggie came to our small California town from Scarsdale, New York, from a prosperous, caring Jewish home and community. She came into our lives as thoroughly not Christian as we thoroughly are. Our Australian daughter, Lynde, introduced her to us. AFS exchange students both (Maggie, domestic; Lynde, foreign), they became best friends in this, the middle of their senior year of high school. Lynde prepared Maggie to meet me by saying, "My mum is a Christian."

"Of course," said Maggie. "Big deal. She is not Jewish."

"No," said Lynde, "I mean, she is really a Christian. I don't mean, non-Jewish, I mean religious." Maggie was baffled. She had never met "really Christian" before, but it was not long before Maggie knew what Lynde meant. We met. I loved her quickly and thoroughly. She was, at sixteen, what she is now, beautiful, dark-eyed, and dark-haired, nonreligious, powerfully opinionated, and powerfully tender. She soon loved me, too. She was intrigued by my faith and we talked about it at great lengths.

I was unaware of internal turmoil that, in part, led Maggie to the West Coast. I did know she spent much of her time with our family. She traveled with us, she ate with us, she laughed, watched TV, and played with us. And, in the Aristotelian sense, Maggie and I enjoyed leisure time together. We grappled with moral and religious issues. All the while, unknown to me, she wrote to her parents about our family, our friendship, our conversations, our discussions of faith.

When the season of exchanges neared an end, Maggie's parents came to retrieve her. We met. We also very much liked each other. We balked at giving Maggie back, we made plans to visit New York, and before long, I found myself there. My first few hours in New York allowed for little more than a quick hello before dressing for a dinner party.

As a West Coast, politically conservative, evangelical Christian, this party was, for me, education. I sat in a beautifully appointed, art-bearing dining room with intelligent, sophisticated, gracious people who knew the merits of wines and the worth of salad greens hitherto unknown to me, with one who had just returned from a meeting with the president of the United States, with bright, liberal people who made things happen. Like a wandering plow horse, I was having a great time plodding in the pasture of tolerant thoroughbreds.

When guests moved to the living room and to individual conversations, Maggie's mother and I settled on a white couch.

At last we had a moment to meet again, to talk to one another. I was not expecting what I got, hot on the heels of hello.

"Maggie loves you very much," she said.

"I love her too. You have a wonderful daughter."

"You know she came to California needing to work out some things. You were such a help to her. I must admit," she continued, "because of your influence, I was afraid you would try to convert her to Christianity. You wouldn't do that, would you?"

I must be honest. I was glad none of my Christian friends were around. I was glad my Bible class women were still on the West Coast and that I was not, even though the next week I told them this story. I needed a moment to breathe, to pray, to think, to weigh my sense of guilt, to respond honestly. My answer satisfied her, but it forced me to see that what I always thought I *should* do in such a circumstance was not what I did when I loaned my life to Maggie. What I *did* was undeniably influenced by these people to whom I was now so affectionately attached. I loaned myself and our home. They affected me.

I answered the question. "Suppose our daughter came to your home, fell in love with your family and you, especially. Like Maggie, suppose Kim was looking for identity and was fascinated by the history and meaning of your family's belief system. If you took advantage of that situation, if you used her distance from us and her trust in you as a catalyst for conversion, as I could have with Maggie, I would be furious with you. Even if you were right, still, I would not respect you. I would not be glad my daughter knew you. I would not respect your religious ideals. I would resent your intrusion, your timing, your lack of restraint or respect for who we are."

I admitted that had Maggie been an adult, had she understood all it meant to step against her own history of connections, of family, and beliefs, and wanted to convert, I would not hesitate to urge her to Christian faith. I am a Christian, after all. But no, I confessed. I could not use her love for me to coerce conviction, to pull her away from all that it means for her to be in her family.

"I didn't think you would" came a gentle reply. Time in New York flew by. Then I began my long journey home. Waiting for me aboard the giant 747 was Guilt. It flew as my uninvited seatmate. It was far more talkative than Nick ever had been and was perfectly armed with certitude.

How hungry Guilt was for my mind and spirit. How ready it was to dominate my time. "How dare you not try to convert Maggie. How dare you admit it! Does her soul not outweigh courtesy to youth, to family? Who cares whether conversion involves advantage, manipulation, a broken sense of respect, or limited understanding of consequences, for goodness sake.

"Good job, Pine. Now go home and teach the Bible study," Guilt said, laying one sharp blow below the belt. "Tell those women what sort of evangelism you practice. Let's see, you can title it 'Hands Off for Jesus.'

"Wanna know why your seat on this flight is so badly located? Why your meal is cold? You do not *deserve* a good seat or hot food! No more blessing-perks for you. You blew it." Ah, the voice of Guilt to born-agains. A pile of "should haves" shouted at me and encouraged shame. I had an enormous amount of sorting to do as a result of loaning my life to Maggie. As much as I affected her, she affected me. She illumined my value system. Obviously, I valued some things above immediate conversion. I valued my responsibility to her family and their trust in ours. I valued the seriousness of conversion. I respected the vulnerability of her youth, my adult advantage, and truth.

Guess what. Down the line Guilt helped me see that I also value my reputation. Even now as I write, I want to admit honestly that loaning affected me. I wish I could write truthfully but avoid censure. Some readers will disapprove of my choice, and that matters to me. Those of us who care about people care about people caring about us!

So, like a bright, new, jacketed book, I loaned myself to Maggie, and now to you. In both cases I come away a bit tattered, maybe even jacketless and, by my choices, less appealing to some. But loaning strengthens me. I have learned. I am not the greatest example of Christian zeal. That is a relief, actually. I confess, in my opinion many current conversion tactics are rude, unloving, thoughtless. A loan to Maggie cemented my respect for dialogue without hidden agendas, for process, for other people's families, for varying points of view. It is quite a challenge to be involved, to be affected, to be faithful. What could be worse? Not to be challenged at all.

Conclusion

In November of 1988 I began writing a specific journal about my friend Linda. The first entry I made was a slightly altered quote from the book by William Maxwell, *So Long, See You Tomorrow*. It seemed to describe her new task perfectly, "Between the way things used to be and the way they were now was a void that couldn't be crossed, a door that shouldn't have been gone through, a place she hadn't meant to leave." Then, I began writing about her. The place she didn't mean to be was on an operating table. One of the earliest pages of what stacked to a hundred said,

The surgeon has opened her from sternum to pubic bone, examined, cut, joined, scoured, biopsied, sutured, bound and released her. . . . The oncologist is now the man to probe, examine, deliberate, recommend, and treat. Cancer is his business, the project of survival is hers.

Well, she has an advantage. Regardless of what else occupies her, Linda finishes projects; potting plants, gathering nature's throw-aways and shaping them into magnificent corner pieces for her house, or arranging books on a shelf in such a way that one wishes to stand forever before them. Somehow, the way Lin "places" things makes a person need to be among them . . . as if we hope her deliberateness will penetrate those of us who love her style but don't know how to make it happen.

During hospitalization, Linda and I decided to ignore the length or frequency of our calls between California and Colorado. A wise decision. I wrote in my journal about a call made the day she left the hospital,

Linda cries in relief, trauma, sadness, fear . . . "I feel so much emotion being back in my home." Merlin, the huge cat, was stretched across her bed with his tongue hanging out. She said, "He looks like I feel." She is ready for humor's relief.

. . . As we work toward a decent time for me to come to Denver, I opted for post-Thanksgiving week. She is recovering wonderfully.

"If I acted as though I am not doing well, would you come sooner?" she asked.

I will. Next Monday. My birthday and the holiday will be spent with her.

. . . Linda is drawing in the turning season. Bare trees stroke

*her emotions, dark skies cushion her bruised mind. The love of
her home holds her up to face the unknown.*

Wednesday, November 16

   *And how am I doing, her friend who plans to fly there, who
will somehow be an anchor in a fierce storm? I am a very "now"
person. Now, I am not crying. That was done last Thursday
through Sunday. Now, I wait. I listen. I am trying to hear Linda
rightly. I need to hear John and her family and doctors and
friends. I need to learn. I am a student of this crisis, being taught
in a language I have only begun to hear. I cannot yet speak it and
I probably only understand one out of every ten or fifteen
words. . . . If I stay long enough and mix well enough with the
inhabitants of this country of cancer, maybe I will hear accurately
and be able to communicate without so many flailing gestures.*

November 23, Wednesday

   *John dozes in the only chair the small examination room
allows. We wait and wait for oncologists. I am perched on a stool
snugged at the corners of Lin's examination table, a large tan
colored metal file cabinet, and a blue and white cardboard box
Lin says holds chemo "throw-aways."*

   *In the interminable waiting period I am struck by everyone's
need to escape this place, this appointment, this truth. Lin is
greatly agitated, frightened, small-talk-chattery.*

   *Doctors finally arrive, discuss, then leave the room and us
with basic facts on a three-page consent form. Linda begins to
read aloud. She does well for a page and a half then control gives
way to tears and heaving sobs as side effects are ticked off:
abdominal cramps, numbness or tingling of fingers and toes,
temporarily paralyzed bowel, severe abdominal pain can occur . . .
nausea, vomiting and diarrhea, increased susceptibility to
infections, bruising and bleeding . . . mouth ulcers and
temporary hair loss, . . . a small but increased risk of leukemia.
Oh, yes, it may also "cause kidney damage."*

"Why bother with all this," Linda asks excruciatingly. "The treatment sounds worse than the disease. I don't want this!"

John holds her, I pat her leg, seated on my stool to her left. We are helpless observers, we cannot be her.

Around 6:00 P.M., under a full harvest moon, we are out of there. Lin and John drive in a car ahead of me. At stop lights I stare at the beautiful, full moon wreathed in a ring of light behind wispy clouds in the black sky. I see my friends silhouetted in their car ahead and cannot believe what we have just experienced. This is a joke, I want to think, as a gut kick connects with my heart and I am awash in sorrow.

That was my birthday. It began at 2:51 A.M., says my journal, when Linda could not sleep, woke me, built a fire, and served me herbal tea (I just cannot learn to like it much). She was swaddled in a dark blue robe, a serape afghan thrown around her shoulders, heavy wool socks, and a knitted ski cap on her head. We laughed at her fashion but bone-deep cold rules her body, and that is not funny. She read to me from her journals about our years of friendship. She cried; we sang a hymn, prayed, and sent her back to bed at about 6:20.

On this day, about twelve hours later, I signed as the witness to my friend's decision to enter a cancer research program. On my birthday she hears the odds for saving her life, signs herself to treatment, begins a journey she did not choose. There is a great void between the way things used to be and are now. Fourteen days have passed since surgery, less than that number stand between her and the beginning of chemotherapy.

I could not sleep through that night. I wondered at a day that marks my life's beginning and marks Lin's dangerous journey ahead. I woke on Thanksgiving Day at 6:20 A.M. wondering how on earth I could possibly be all I ought to be in this most unwelcome process. I was terrified, but the terror brought with it a most important realization. I began to write. My journal records,

Dearest Linda;

I am not God. I cannot be a shield or a fortress. But I promise to be a wall for you against which you can lean for as long as the bricks of this wall hold together.

But I am not God. I wish I were. But, you may lean . . . to the extent of my strength.

Between November 1988 and July 1990 I learned about loaning my life to Linda. I learned about limitations: Mine. I learned about friendship: Ours. I learned about giving, whether or not it gets rewarded or whether or not it changes anything. I learned how good it is to surrender freedom, to give without expectations and with no demands. Linda gave, too. Nobly, much of the time. She helped me learn the art of loaning. What a final gift. Yes?

CHAPTER
SIX

*L*aughing

Not far from my desk stands a shelf of books that rescue me when I tire from swimming in my deep pool of ignorance. Some are about philosophy and philosophers. I appreciate this discipline but just cannot keep its periods and problems straight in my mind. I can't remember what Kant could, I discarded Descartes when I realized one must be a mathematician to follow his reasoning, and while I have great regard for Kierkegaard, I simply lack the *a*ability to track through *a*all that gr*aa*ve German philosophy he understands in his d*aa*rk, D*aa*nish way.

As composers do, philosophers win my admiration. But if admiration requires remembering who said or wrote what in which century, I falter. I simply cannot remember. With one exception: Voltaire.

I remember Voltaire because while reading work by him and about him, I laughed. Voltaire was an eighteenth-century Frenchman impressed with the English and usually in trouble with authorities in Paris. Because of him, I remember yet another, slightly earlier philosopher, Gottfried Leibniz. I recall a seminary professor mentioning him and learning then that German diphthongs get the sound of the second vowel. From seminary I learned to say correctly, Leibniz. But I remember what Leibniz believed and what Voltaire thought of it because I laughed.

Not humorously, Leibniz explained our world in terms of substances and strivings and sufficient reason, and concepts and consequences *far* beyond my comprehension. He theorized that ours is the best possible world. God, he says, created it precisely *as* it is because as it *is,* it is the best of all possible worlds. I vaguely recall a discussion of this in my hermeneutics class. You can, no doubt, understand my never giving it a thought once grades were rewarded. That is, until I borrowed a copy of Voltaire's *Candide.*

I must have been goldbricking or ice skating while during my youth others were reading classics. But last winter, having finished the book I brought along and needing something to read in the short time of vacation remaining, I browsed among my daughter-in-law's books. There stood *Candide.* Obviously a classic, it was small and worn. Courtney said, "You haven't read *Candide?* It's great." Perfect. I picked it up and began at the introduction. Thank goodness for introductions, they serve as language instructors for those of us unfamiliar with the classical tongue. I learned quickly that Voltaire not only created characters, he was one. I laughed from the start when André Maurois introduced Voltaire as

a dying man: he had been one all his life. But in his health, about which he was for ever complaining, he had a valuable prop which he used to wonderful advantage: for Voltaire's constitution was robust enough to withstand the most extreme mental activity, yet frail enough to make any other excess difficult to sustain.

Selectively excessive himself, Voltaire responded to an era fraught with excesses by thrusting a sense of humor rather than the usual sword. For instance, by playfully constructing his tomb half inside the church and half in the graveyard at his Ferney estate, he symbolized his conviction that the "rascals" of the church "will say I'm neither in nor out." He approved of God but abhorred and discounted superstition abounding in the church. He was a deist but kept a Jesuit father in residence at his retreat home (read exiled home) in Ferney, near Geneva.

Voltaire deplored the despotism of nobility so common to his world and did something about it. The hamlet of Ferney and the lives of common people there were transformed by his establishing industry and commerce. He allowed religious tolerance. He provided homes for the townspeople, developed a center for the making of fine watches and lace, and employed workers in his own massive gardens and orchards. He was convinced that work "keeps us from three great evils: boredom, vice, and poverty."

I am not capable of essaying the good or evil contributed by Voltaire. I am not a philosopher, not a judge of any. I can only say that he won from me what no other philosopher has, my memory. His opposition to Leibniz, his sense of the futility of idle optimism, his strong advocacy of positive action and work all settled in my mind as if they belong there. Voltaire made me listen by making me laugh. *Candide* is a *very* funny book, a bawdy but fine satire. In it Voltaire hurled accurately a weapon for minimizing opposition, for driving home a point, winning an audience, relieving frustration, easing tension, expressing humility, exercising power. His weapon? Humor. Or, if you prefer, and the English do, humour.

Hail Humour

Until the eighteenth century, humour came in four colors: red, yellow, black, and green. The word belonged to the world of medicine and represented four body fluids, the balance of which determined a person's temperament, mood, and health. Theory held that humours—blood, phlegm, yellow bile, black bile—released spirits or vapors that affected the brain. We still nod to that ancient idea when we say, "green with envy," or speak of a "black mood." Yellow is the color of jonquils, yes, but of cowards, too.

It took centuries for the meaning of humour to shift to "ho-ho-ho." For that delay, either blame or congratulate the ancient Romans and Greeks who planted strong roots of opinion. They drove deep the conviction that "ho-ho-ho" rises from shabbiness (and some does). Back in the B.C.'s, Plato considered humour a scoffing response to things weak. Aristotle, so wise on leisure, disdained laughter, arguing that it required a base of defect. Oh, those philosophers to whom we pay so little attention, always drawing conclusions with which we find ourselves living, unawares. Of course philosophers deliberated more admirably than my broad-stroke picture paints here, but generally speaking, their ancient ideas marched directly, and unassaulted, into the Middle Ages. While doctors of that period were using the word humour, no one expressed any. Society agreed that open laughter was inappropriate; it projected signs of superior feelings, signaled self-glorification. Nix it. Eighteenth-century Lord Chesterfield did, in correspondence to his son: "there is nothing so illiberal, and so ill-bred, as audible laughter," he wrote. But consider. What was there to laugh about, given a history of barbarians, crusades, earthquakes, plagues, lice, and cholera, yes?

Dave Barry, Garrison Keillor, beware. Till nearly yesterday, laughter represented a "vacant mind," was regarded as sinister behavior, called the "hiccup of a fool," or a sneeze in good sense. Humour experts of the past, like the tobacco industry of today, maintained a convincing but faulty opinion. Then, between the sixteenth and eighteenth centuries, changes stirred. Playwrights saw new opportunity in prevailing thought. They created "humours" works. That is, comedy based on the four humours. Ben Jonson was the first, with his 1598 off-Broadway hit, *Every Man in His Humour.* The popularity of this emerging genre, the spinning of tales of imbalanced humours, produced a gradual language shift. Humour slipped off medical charts and landed in the midst of society as a description of something causing us to laugh. Audibly. Actually, before long the old usage was double cursed. Not only playwrights but scientists tampered with the status quo. Modern medicine was born and screeched directly into the ear of ancient medical theory, deafening its senses. Sound health, it proved, was not a product of balancing colorful body fluids. Now, what else could be done with the word *humour* but make it hilarious? Its original usage certainly proved so.

Today, of course, the value of "ho-ho-ho" is medically, psychologically, and even intellectually appreciated as a sign of health, wit, and well-being. Unless assigned to diabolical or cruel use, laughter is a positive means of minimizing opposition, of driving home a point, of winning an audience, of relieving frustration, of breaking tension, of expressing humility, of cementing love, or, of exercising power. Let us hail humour, or humor, as the Americans prefer. And oh, yes, when we discuss healthy humour, one indispensable element bubbles at its center. That is, the element of surprise.

Prize Surprise

Arthur Schopenhauer, of the early nineteenth century and another of those interminable philosophers, said correctly that laughter occurs when we recognize incongruity. Good. But then at the close of the nineteenth century and before Darwin became the star of such things, evolutionist Herbert Spencer proposed that incongruity fostered a downward movement. The "conscious is unawares transferred from great things to small," he stated. That, I suppose, seemed not funny to a social evolutionist. Not good. But at least incongruity, *things out of keeping, out of place, or out of agreement,* got recognized as that which tickles us. It makes us laugh. It distracts us from "great" things.

Freud tossed a psychological faggot or two onto the crackling discussion. Other than my knowing that the German diphthong theory breaks down in the pronunciation of his name, I know little about Freud. Still, I thank him for noticing that humour grants relief from unpleasant emotion and that it is among the most important human emotional defenses. There is no question but that pressures of real life require a defense or two. It is a fine thing to learn that laughter nearly always accompanies humour, and that both prove psychologically and physiologically good for us.

But humour does not have to accompany laughter. Only an element of surprise, massive or minuscule, does. We laugh when our minds or emotions are snoozing, when the incongruous strikes our thinking. Whether it is something we see, hear, taste, touch, or smell, if that *something* is unexpected even to a slight degree, we are inclined to laugh. And laugh we do. Laugh we must, to be authentic, to be real. We must prize surprise, for from it we gain blips and basketsful of joyous reprieve. Please, turn the page to see what I saw recently.

This page intentionally left blank.

I hope you smiled some as you puzzled over the page you just turned. Only yesterday I came upon three pages like it as I scanned a financial report. The report proved generally boring, full of figures I failed to understand. But, when I came to those "blank" pages I cracked up. Maybe practiced readers of boring reports expect such things, but they completely surprised me. I enjoyed the incongruity so much I saved a page.

Having to tell a reader not to worry about a blank page, that's good. The report compilers probably felt as I did in chapter five, "If you write us, do not write asking about this. The page is intentionally blank." But best, of course, is that the page is *not* blank. Ludicrous? Yes. Incongruous? Yes. Funny? At least to me. Maybe all reports should require their monotony broken with an occasional unblank blank page, a "Far Side" cartoon, a Dave Barry or P. J. O'Rourke quote. Surprise! Laughter. Ah, such a pleasant reprieve.

Real people laugh a lot, but that may be among the hardest lessons for conscientious people to learn. They so seriously approach life, after all. Perhaps we all need reminding that conscientious people are not necessarily authentic people. Any of us can conscientiously commit to artificial behavior, to inappropriate attitudes, or to uncalled-for sobriety. Real people laugh a lot because they have learned three hard lessons. They know that:

- We all make major and minor mistakes worth laughing at.
- Things we hold dear are worthy of laughter.
- Our selves are significant, but also hilarious.

Surprise: Real People Make Mistakes

Real people let go. They laugh a lot, and they love life when they do. They are not guilty of treating surprise, incongruity, or mishap as evidence of personal failure. Mistakes score our adaptability and, if handled well, make us bearable. Small example: my friend who entered the wrong restroom in a restaurant. She swiftly retraced her steps, saying, "Oops, a woman's restroom just doesn't have those cute wall fixtures!"

What a surprise! And what a gift to those of us with her there. Her "mistake" allowed us all to get healthier as we nearly rolled under the table recalling wrong restroom moments. All people make mistakes, but real people have great fun with them. Well, with some of them.

I have made major mistakes. I mean major, the sort not at all immediately funny, some never so. There are mistakes that simply cannot jump the fence of funny. But I am also old enough now to realize that there is little that does not eventually slip into humor's yard. The Holocaust does not. Drunk driving does not. Drunks may do some funny things, but drunk is not funny. But perhaps it is not fair to place those things in the category of mistakes. A mistake is *an error in action, calculation, opinion, or judgment caused by poor reasoning, carelessness, or insufficient knowledge, etc.*

Deliberate cruelty or evil is not a laughing matter, but mistakes nearly always become so. I wish, as a first soprano in a choir concert, I had not bellowed out an entrance one-fourth of a beat before the sheet music beckoned voices. I wish that especially for my friend Karen the choir director, and for her husband as well, who so expertly recorded it all. But enter early I did. And that mistake, much sooner than I thought it ought, invited my friends and family to sympathetic but unrestrained laughter.

I wish I had not made the mistake of waxing poetic on a final theology class exam. My professor, a brilliant, no-nonsense scholar whose real name I will refrain from using since I highly respect him, wrote at the top of my many pages of essay, "What *happened* to you?" He proceeded throughout the pages of my rambling thoughts to insist I had "*not* learned this" from him.

Whoa! What a mistake. I thought I faithfully wrote back what I learned from him, but, after I swallowed the shocking D affixed to that final exam, and gave thanks for the B on the course where A's once reigned, I began to laugh. After a day or two, I let others laugh with me. I wrote a whimsical poem to assuage the pain. It helps keep me laughing.

The Death of a 3.5 GPA

Dr. Winston Master's "D,"
I got it.
By first-class mail it came to me.
  I'm not convinced I earned the grade,
  I know the effort I had made
  to write a decent final.

But Dr. Winston Master's "D"
reminded me that
  Effort is not all that needs
  to hit the desk
  of busy Educators;
  scholared, quick Evaluators
    of every student's skill.

The work for Dr. Master's desk
(In my case graded as a mess)
    should be an echo of the best;
    like that of Dr. Winston Master.

My work must ring of scholarship
should sound true tones of Mentor's lips;
    must call to his precisioned mind
    those times he made all truth clear.

Oh, dear! I wrote far too poetically,
my 3.5 is history,
    I earned myself a shocking "D"
    from Dr. Winston Master.

In answer to the disappointed professor, I do not know what happened to me on that test. I found my work less objectionable than did he. I justified for myself that its content did bob along somewhere between the banks of flowing historical accuracy. But, I admit, I wrote much too poetically, took too many liberties where my knowledge ran into unknown eddies, and obviously frustrated my most precise professor. In short, I made a terrible mistake. The resultant grade shredded my dream of scholarship, but in the long run, it made my seminary memory more colorful than expected. It made me laugh.

So did an encounter with a fellow student at the Catalyst, the campus coffee shop. This time the mistake was his, but we shared the laugh. I stood waiting for coffee and suffering the effects of my Intensive Greek class. I felt ancient and stupid and sorry for myself, a normal attitude as I prepared for midterms. Who *cares* about cases, declensions, participles, forms, or agreeing endings. While I put in the fifty or so study hours it took each week to earn twelve units, my honestly-great instructor watched a whimsical PBS series by Douglas

Adams. Each morning he faithfully opened class with an accurate report of the last night's hilarious episode and asked the truly unfair question, "Did you watch?"

That was the state of things. Now, I stood waiting for coffee, trying to remember why I thought seminary was so wonderful, when a man with whom I once shared a class struck up a conversation. Soon, apparently noticing a glint from my gesturing left hand, he said, "Oh no. You're *mar*ried." To my wondering why that was a problem, he said, "I was going to ask you for a date."

Well, hey! Thank goodness for life's surprises. What a nice mistake. Actually, he was too young for me anyway and, sadly, too old for my then single daughter. But he was just right for a moment that needed laughter. He was a good sport. We all make major and minor mistakes, but perhaps the biggest we make in all sorts of settings is that of not laughing soon enough. All people make mistakes. Real people have fun with them.

Things Dear to Us Are Worthy of Laughter

Real people respect the significance of being but do not turn to pillars of salt if they occasionally turn away from it. Significant things, ideas, and being, are kept at ease by authentic people. Dr. Jim Bradley, my mentor and formerly my history professor at Fuller Seminary, sets a great example. Dr. Bradley, who students say "looks a lot like Jesus," is an incredible blend of scholarship, spiritual depth, and humility. I suppose the places where he sometimes is required to lecture have added to his practiced humility. For instance, Early Church History met in a large, old basement room where noisy, exposed plumbing pipes ran along the low ceiling and where an elevator to who-knows-where-but-not-here, opened near the professor's lectern and always to the surprise of occupants. Always to the delight of a hundred or so gawking class members.

One class day, as he frequently did, Dr. Bradley made a brilliant statement. The class, as it usually did, hushed, to absorb the wisdom of this man's thought. But unexpectedly, a sudden rushing noise yanked our attention ceiling-ward. The next sound was Dr. Bradley saying, "Every time I say something profound they flush the toilet upstairs."

Hooray! Dr. Bradley is real. He knows weighty moments can bear laughter. His own dear thought held up well under humor. We do not plan to laugh at important things, only we find ourselves in situations where important things as well as important selves are subject to surprise. Incongruity does not necessarily turn minds from great things to small, as Spencer insisted, but rather it allows great things to remain great while we take a small break to notice a moment of surprise, a perfectly presented opportunity to laugh. Take it. That is my advice.

Recently I was lecturing a gathering of community college personnel. Picture this. At the head table, I sat left of the lectern. Next to me was the college president. On the other side of the lectern sat the chancellor of colleges, and to her right sat my husband, David, who accepted the invitation to join me at this breakfast meeting.

Normally, David hears my speeches before they reach any audience. But not in this case. Here, he listened, like everyone else, for the first time. Well, it is not fair to say, he listened *like* everyone else. He did not. He listened like a husband. At least, like mine. My lecture's introduction quoted a dialogue Bill Cosby imagined between Noah and God. It set up a question I intended to investigate: "Who is this really?" At about the third line of exchange, I said, "And Noah said,"

"No, honey, you mean, 'Cosby said,'" said my dear husband from the chancellor's side, genuinely unaware of what he was doing.

Shall I make an understatement? The eyes of the crowded room moved to the handsome, gray-haired man with the bright red face. They were interested in who it was correcting their guest speaker. Dave worked at disappearing. In the hush of this moment I said, "Ladies and gentlemen, I would like to introduce my husband, David, who finds it necessary, even here, to correct me." We all started laughing. This was literally an "incredible" moment. David rose to his feet. Holding a cloth napkin over the nodding head held between his hands, he attempted to apologize. Laughter only grew greater as his embarrassment struggled for acquittal. Men howled; women wiped tears from their eyes. If there had been any question, this moment answered it. This audience and I were now solid friends. What a splendid punctuation this laughter allowed. No, not punctuation, puncturation. Laughter wonderfully punctures any distorted sense of a moment's worth, or any soaring sense of self-importance. If we let it.

Authenticity is not manufactured by a mood or a setting; it is carried in character. Perfect settings do not a masterpiece make, although ideal settings do them justice. Masterpieces deserve good settings but are not guaranteed them. They are sometimes stored in basements, attics, stashed away and neglected. Masterpieces of human character appreciate perfect settings, too. But people seldom have the luxury of ideal settings. Real people laugh about dear things and in dear moments. Even things and moments that hurt us.

Linda was dear to me. For twenty-six years we cherished our friendship. We truly loved each other. On the first trip I made to be with her during her final hospitalization, we affixed a "do not disturb" sign to the door, unplugged the phone, told the nurses no visitors, then stretched out on her bed together to talk.

We began seriously. We asked ourselves if there was any unfinished business between us. We knew the possibility that Linda was dying. Anything unfinished? Needing discussion? Explained? Then the laughter began because we were plainly surprised by the silence that answered our intense questions. This friendship was very well tended. That surprised us. It should not have, but did. And you know what we did? We laughed.

We allowed ourselves to follow our resting heads back in memory. We laughed over the day we decided "to heck with public opinion." When we met one another in airports, we hugged joyously and shared a kiss. We often held hands as we walked through corridors, so happy to see one another. We laughed over friendship having to calculate its public behavior. We laughed at our own daring.

We very nearly winded ourselves that day in the hospital, laughing over the memory of Linda—soft, Texan Linda—pursuing a deliberately rude driver down a freeway. Having enough of his behavior, she succeeded in forcing him to the side of the road where she stood by his window shaking her finger under his nose and over his dropped jaw; scolding him, hot Texas style in the cold Colorado snow. No one can spout expletives quite like an enraged Texas woman, we agreed. She cringed in memory. We laughed, hard.

We cried hard too. We hated that her life was waning. We hated the terror ahead. This life-loving woman trusted well that God knew what He was doing, but she did not have to like it. Ah, how real. How funny, her moments of handling fear in that hospital room. She created more than one obnoxious scene in the middle of the night, in order to draw people to her bedside. Only when we figured how the possibility of dying alone frightened her was it arranged for people to share her room during the deepest hours of night's fear.

I remember gladly that Linda and I spent nearly as much time laughing as we did crying, even as we prayed. The time came where laughter no longer fit. But, while it did, it fed us relief, fetched memories for conversations, strengthened our love, and delivered us for as long as it could from the sorrow ahead. Dear, dear things, dear people. God protect us, from fearing the nobility of laughter.

Our Very Selves Are Not Only Significant but Are Hilarious

I am not glad that in the last two years, highly significant people have died. This year my grandmother, Linda in July of 1990, and the following June, friend Cal Gregg. My grandmother was abundantly witty, but Cal was simply the funniest man around. He never forgot a joke, and he never failed to tell it well. He was an Irishman with a powerfully dark side, but his humor challenged it with brightness. Till he slipped into a coma, Cal rose out of the most dreadful moments of pain or anguish with a witty or humorous aside. Laughter was his constant gift to those of us who walked with him through that strange valley of death. His life was significant. He absolutely did not want it to finish. He wanted years with his eldest son's child. He wanted to see his younger son through high school. The significance of being, of treasuring life could not have been more firmly felt by anyone. But Cal never ceased to squeeze humorous pleasure from significance. Many of us would massage his tumor-rippled back in wee hours of the night. One night, finding himself hilarious and me much too inclined toward a maudlin mood, he said, "The good thing about losing all this weight is that my friends can work on my back and I feel it in front, too!"

A favorite of his stories concerns the day his arm broke. By the time this happened cancer had vigorously infiltrated every cranny of his body. Still, he fought. He went to work as often as he could, even for a few hours at a time. He attended Grapple Group, where between shuffles to the bathroom to allow the sickness of chemotherapy to have its say, he contributed, listened to others, cared about what was going on, asked about the rest of us. He still had moments of planning to conquer cancer. Then his arm broke.

A back door to his small business warehouse required a little tug up to close properly. We all do that little yank occasionally, to some door or other. But in this light lift, Cal's arm shattered. Cancer made its effect clear. How much more can he take, I thought. How discouraging, I thought. And it was. Poor Cal, I thought, till I went to see him after X-rays.

"Sue needs to pray more specifically," he said.

"What?" I wondered. Sue Hendrix is the friend who established F.O.G. She was one of several nurses who helped Cal regularly and faithfully.

"Well, yeah," he said. "You know how she prayed, 'Lord, give Cal a break.'"

Goodness, how we laughed! What does it mean when a dying friend tousles *your* hair, or your expectations, helps you relax, recognizes his significance but never ceases to remember that being human has a hilarious side, equally as precious as the serious side.

In certain turnings of truth, being human is hilarious. It is such a brief, precious, and mysterious thing. We are basically bright but in so many ways helpless and hapless, so out of touch with nature's instinctual creatures. Especially those of us called civilized. We are solidly incapable of ever "always" doing it right, whatever "it" is. We cannot even agree on what is good for us to eat, let alone on theologies, or policies, or means of peace. So serious are we about frivolous things and so frivolous about serious things.

How glad I am that God understands the whole while I struggle with the pieces. Laughter regularly reminds me that we are only human, but that we are *truly* human. No other species has the blessing of such sensitive self-awareness or the gift of sophisticated laughter. No other, the burden of keeping those things on an even keel. A commitment to laughter, a respect for its place among significant selves, helps keep us real.

Conclusion

"It will never work," my grandfather declared one particular day in my childhood. His son-in-law and my father, Chas, was placing heavy cream in a thermos-like cola maker. It belonged to my grandfather, and in its normal use a CO_2 cartridge acted on a cola syrup and water with delicious results. No so CO_2 on heavy cream, we soon learned. As my stern "I-told-you-so" grandfather looked on and said, "Boy Howdy," as he often did, the experiment exploded—up, on the ceiling. But well clabbered, I remember. Pop's triumphal display of disapproval only intensified our laughter. We simply could not look up without collapsing into laughter. The more Pop shook his head, the louder he protested with his familiar "Mmmm-unnn," and the more he called for control, the less we managed it. My parents, my grandmother, her children my age, my brother, and I were conquered by surprise. What a great mistake! What a dear mess! What a hilarious sight we significant people produced. My grandfather was a character there in his all-knowing authority, but the group around him that day displayed an element *of* human character that simply must not be squelched—laughter.

*L*eaving

People regularly leave places, situations, growth plateaus, habits, relationships, interests, experiences, preferences, feelings, ideas, and life. Obviously, the process of living is one that beats a natural rhythm of arriving and leaving, attaching and separating. Authentic living virtually requires surrender to the rhythm but, also, a commitment to managing its effect. All people leave things, but too few leave deliberately or well.

Some leavings occur so naturally and so slowly that transitions require no notice. For instance, childhood speech patterns. When, we wonder years later, did Edward stop saying "Bay-oh" and start saying "Bear"? When did he leave toddler talk? Some leavings are abrupt, jarring, and full of notice. Anger, illness, political shifts, passions of religion or romance often trigger swift exits, sudden releases, or hard separations.

Leavings, gentle or harsh, are as plentiful as hair on our bodies; some, as bothersome as hair in our mouths. But if we want leavings to help us shape fine character, we learn to tend them, like hair on a show cat. *Leave: to go out of or away from.*

Separate. Depart. Take off. Change. Scram. That does *not* say, be ejected, expelled, booted, or other embarrassing removals that can occur. These are passive words, they describe things done *to* us. But to leave means to exercise volition. Even if asked to leave, we make the move. We are not asked, "Please be ejected." Leave is a responsibility word.

Imagine a trapeze artist propelled toward change. He releases a swiftly receding swing, hangs unsupported for a split second, then clutches a new opportunity. Seldom are our daily separations so dramatic, but leaving requires actively letting go of this in order to take hold of that. Wise trapezists avoid carelessness; they train and practice. They know leaving is serious business, that life depends upon it. It does, in a real sense, for all of us. Then why is deliberate leaving so neglected? So difficult? I think for at least these three reasons: 1) a need to be sure, 2) a need to feel safe, and 3) a reluctance to be sad.

The Need to Be Sure

Even when we think we know, leaving usually means being unsure of what is next. A postcard I saw recently says it best.

> "Piglet sidled up to Pooh from behind.
>   'Pooh!' he whispered.
>   'Yes, Piglet?'
>   'Nothing,' said Piglet, taking Pooh's paw.
>   'I just wanted to be sure of you.'"

Taking Pooh's paw, wanting to "be sure of." How familiar. Nearly everyone wishes for a "Pooh's paw" before going on, whether going on is off a diving board for the first time or off to college. Whether leaving is ordinary or dramatic, it sure helps to be sure.

As a child I puzzled over adults in our church who were *so sure of* Heaven's floorplan that they spoke longingly of leaving, of being "with the Lord." I was in no hurry to go to heaven. I still am not. There was a time when I worried that my hesitancy to leave indicated a lack of faith. Then I grew smarter.

First, I recognized that some of what I had heard was rhetoric. Much leaving talk is just that, talk. Children create leaving talk well: "I don't care if we have to go. I don't like this place anyway. I never really wanted to come here." Language of that sort convinces children (and some adults) that leaving is preferred to staying. It is an infantile but effective way of coping, in the modern sense of the word *cope*. They have not yet learned to separate well or how to treasure memories. But adults are better off knowing better.

As a youngster, I noticed that some leave-talking adults, when given the actual opportunity to fly heavenward, vigorously declined, instead clung tenaciously to hearth and health. Ah, clearly, it is an *idea* of leaving that gets hugged to the heart! Leaving is a good idea, but its exercise is a different matter. Like the frequent brisk walks we all need, it is easy to avoid when we are comfortable where we are.

As an adult I realize that I am basically comfortable where I am. Where some songwriters and eager-leavers see "dreary sod," I see fertile earth and Kingfishers diving for dinner. I smell the fragrance of Solomon's Seal or orange blossoms, or see lives changed by faith, or by courage, or by help from people who loan themselves. The truth is, I am mostly satisfied here and seldom is anyone motivated to leave what seems good—even when it is a bad thing.

I am not weary enough for a world-leaving. I do not suffer deprivation of food or shelter as many of earth's inhabitants do. Even the worst members of my family are basically nice people. My mind and body are reasonably healthy, my pains seem surmountable, and so far at least, grace comforts more than sin condemns. I like knowing God, here, where I am comfortable and feel relatively sure of things.

Anselm, I think, would understand. A great medieval theologian and Benedictine monk, Anselm was born the son of a priest in Italy and died in England serving as the Archbishop of Canterbury. Anselm was as brilliant as his travel was broad. Much of his time was spent forwarding "necessary reasons" for things concerning the existence of God. As nearly as I can tell, Anselm liked being "sure of" things.

If this were a chapter on philosophical theology we would investigate his Ontological Argument which seeks to define divine realities. It is impossible to remember Anselm without acknowledging his great contribution to Christology, the Satisfaction Theory of Atonement. But in my reading about Anselm, I got hooked by a very personal moment in his life, by his behavior at the time of leaving, by his desire to be sure.

On April 21, 1109, Anselm died. It was a Wednesday before Easter Sunday. Apparently on Palm Sunday, his friends tried to help him "leave." One said,

"Father and Lord, as far as it is given to us to know, you are leaving this world and are going to keep the Easter Court with our Lord."

Anselm, in his gracious way, replied, "If it is His will I shall gladly obey, but if He should prefer me to stay with you just long enough to solve the question of the origin of the soul which I have been turning over in my mind, I would gratefully accept the chance, for I doubt that anybody else will solve it while I am gone." (L. Russ Bush, Editor, *Classical Readings in Christian Apologetics*)

When my gentle grandmother died, she wanted to leave life. She was ninety-three years worth of ready. Linda did not want to leave, nor did Cal. Anselm did not. Four people of sure faith. When I think of people I knew who died before their ideas tired, I remember few, regardless of a state of assurance, who wanted to leave. Anselm, believer extraordinaire, was not "sure" that anyone else would care as he did about the origin of the soul. In all fairness, do you know the soul's origin or anyone who seriously inquires after it? Seldom do I see sign-up sheets for groups dedicated to its discovery. "I would gratefully accept the chance. . ." For what—to stay here? Here, where my ideas fit, where I am more sure of things. So would most of us, Anselm, in many situations, not just at death.

Leavings produce concerns as quickly as a magician pulls silk scarves from a bouquet of flowers. Wanting to be sure of things before we embrace them is often instantly followed by a concern for safety. David and I had not been out of California for more than two days before my need to feel safe said, "I want to go home."

Ah, the Need to Be Safe

It is true that on our recent journey to Washington State our rolling profile resembled something out of *The Grapes of Wrath*. Our aging BMW was so loaded down that the trunk refused to latch till David removed two clothes hangers. Atop the car a ski rack was filled-to-sky-high with household goods by blue (ugly) plastic tarps then drawn taut by crisscrossing ropes protecting all from wind, rain, and, we hoped, collapse. The picture is not yet complete. Attached behind the beige car and loaded to the limits of the law a wooden utility trailer rolled jauntily on wheels so ancient and massive it required a county search to find balloon tires that fit them. I suspect FDR and the CCC constructed that old trailer. Oh yes, color it sugar-mint green.

As if this whizzing distraction needed intensifying (as if all this could whiz), we carried along two large dogs. Born who-knows-where and each rescued as pups from animal shelters, our somewhat-golden retriever and our dubiously-black lab rested, stood, slept, and played in the back half of the two-door vehicle atop more packed goods, tail tips brushing the rear window, noses to our shoulders. Those who understand current Northwestern prejudices can appreciate that to some we not only looked evil, we surely were, for we were tacked together, front and back, by California license plates. Only a flyer announcing a Communist cell meeting and nailed to a telephone pole on the Baptist church grounds in the 1950s could have earned more contempt. Mercifully, that truth had not yet dawned on us. We felt good about this leaving, we were "sure of" this move until we reached Portland, Oregon.

There, David recalled a remarkable site, a beautiful hotel lobby. He was not sure where it was but thought he could find it and wanted me to see it. He finds things well—not in the house or in his pockets—only in distant cities or from the sky. But not this time. We drove to the city center, searched, failed, and aimed again for the freeway. This leaving required a few busy intersections, and one particular red light. At it we stopped, dutifully. As it turned green and we turned left, the driver behind us honked. David and I exchanged glances. Were our lights on? No. Had something fallen from the car? Apparently not. Had we lingered too long at the light? Not at all. The street we entered allowed the honking car to move up beside us. In a matter of seconds my concern for emotional safety emerged full-grown.

The confronting car (Oregon-licensed-vehicle-of-war) held two women—one rather grandmotherly, in the old-fashioned sense, and a middle-aged driver I supposed was her daughter. Whoever, they jockeyed to a position paralleling us where the gray-haired passenger proceeded to make exaggerated faces at us. This is true. Hilarious in retrospect, but shocking at the time. *You* picture it.

A smile takes about sixteen muscles, a frown forty-three; the human body has only 656 muscles all told. But this woman, I swear to you, worked at least a thousand muscles against us that day. She used them all in a time's flash and with a most practiced manner to convey anger, hatred, disdain, intolerance, and childishness. I was dumbstruck. A city block and an eternity rolled past. Both cars were forced to slow down for another red light. David smiled. I saw it coming, I begged him, "Please do *not* get involved in this. David, plee-ze . . ." So much for my influence.

Energetically he signaled the woman, "Lower your window."

"No!" she shook her head wildly. But perplexity slipped obviously onto her agile face. Somehow her missile of intimidation failed to destroy, even injure, the enemy. While she grappled for new strategy David fired a huge smile her way. Bull's eye! In spite of herself, she *was* curious. What *is* this strange Californian going to do next? He was meant to cringe (like his wife); he was to wither when hit. Rather, he invited exchange. She fell for it. She rolled down her window while an exaggerated planting of her shoulders and head inferred grave resistance. "Notice, you prune-pickers," she conveyed, "nary an inch of give!" Both cars stopped completely. I prayed for a miracle, "Change light, now!" So much for my influence; we waited.

"You'll be happy to know we're moving here!" hollered David, across the line of fire.

"You know you're NOT WELCOME!" she countered, bullying but unable to completely mask the shock delivered by this man's unpredictable nerve.

"I know," he responded, joyfully. "But, we're moving *here,* and we're bringing all our friends and family from California with us!" Oh, how he laughed. The light changed, on schedule. The "ladies" left. The dogs stood and wagged tails, sensing something wonderful in the air. How that man I married did enjoy that moment of . . . of what? I cannot call it noble character. I will not call it commitment to excellence. But, I suppose, I must call it a moment of being real. So authentic was he. And I? Oh, my response was sterling. Eyes downcast, I continued knitting. That is, I entrapped and paralyzed my fingers in an increasingly harsh tangle of yarn. "Get me out of this city," I begged. "Please leave." I am not much fun when I am not safe. I cried some.

The freeway restored a modicum of security, or at least a measure of anonymity. As my shock and tears diminished I said something like, "Are we not citizens of the United States? Is this city not a city within the United States? Did we *do* something to deserve that treatment?" We chewed hard on a discussion of being objects of discrimination. Not who we were personally but that we were where they did not want us determined the reaction to us of perfect strangers. Well, not "perfect" strangers. Perhaps those Portland women are decent, but I will not call them perfect, in any respect. But who they are is not the point. Leaving is. It can feel unsafe, it can be unsafe, even when we tend it well.

We let go of California, hung for a split second in Portland, and quickly attached to Washington. Day one: purchase local license plates and cut down chances of harassment. Then, because we fully intended to stay, we built the dogs' fence, ordered the newspaper, and arranged for local banking. We signed on dotted lines for savings, checking, and Visa accounts here, at a small branch of a proud state bank. You know the sort, where local business people walk in to make deposits at the end of the day, where neighbors wave and chat as they stand in line to make a transaction, where people know one another's names, where tellers smile and good things happen. As they did for us, in our small California town, in our local bank there, even though we did not say that here, where talk of California is slow to grow warm.

Ah, yes. The noble Northwest. Where good people live well. Where even before the ink dried on the new checks from our new bank, some new, perfect stranger "borrowed" our account number and successfully forged their way to several hundred of our dollars. Of course the bank made good our loss. It also decided to close the transgressed account and open us a *new* new one. That decision was executed, post-haste. But, in the split seconds between leaving and attaching, between accounts old and new, unexpected things can happen. And do. The bank unintentionally botched an arrangement for paying the checks still circulating from the *old* new account. Consequently, before too many days passed it appeared that the Pines were bouncing checks from one end of the country to the other. Ah, but our bank bounced back. They wrote letters of explanation and apology; they assumed the cost of their errors. They apologized; they solved the problems. All but one. A local one. Rising in a bakery.

The check I wrote, paying for several loaves of tasty bread made in a small bakery in this fine harbor community, came from the now defunct first account. It bounced and was returned by the bank to the bakery stamped, "SUSPECTED FORGERY." Great. Naturally, it carried my name, my local phone number, and the bold numbers of my California driver's license. Mr. Local Baker was not happy. He did not know that fault lay with the bank where he too transacts business and chats with old friends. He called me. He set his tone as the woman in Portland set her shoulders. As he made his point I very much regretted leaving our home in California, where the sun and the people are warm.

"I don't know what kind of community you *come* from," he said, instructing me, "but these sorts of things do not happen *here*."

I know that in a commitment to being real, people *work* to relate well to others but do not always succeed. That day, I venture, I did not. I tightened my own tone and coolly informed him that, in fact, we came from a community quite similar in size to this one, had lived there for twenty-five years, and could assure him this "sort of thing" never happened to us *there*. I encouraged him to call his fine bank—*here*—where these sorts of things never happen, but did.

As I write, I truly wish The Baker knew the rest of our story. Not only did someone use our checking account illegally, but our new local bank-issued credit card number got used by someone we do not know to purchase expensive concert seats. Probably the tickets were used. The Visa card no longer can be. That account, like the checking account, was closed and reopened under a *new* new number.

Shortly thereafter, on the way home from church, we stopped at a Seattle bakery, where even *better* bread is baked, and while we selected como and sourdough rye, some industrious citizen ripped off emblems, front and back, from our BMW. Not in eight years of driving that car in California did anyone do so vile a thing. Ah, these wonderful Puget Sounders, just people, like those we left behind. The point, of course, is not that northwesterners suffer unfairly the invasion of outsiders or that we outsiders discover a particularly nasty streak in northwesterners. The point here is that leavings carry the forfeiture of guaranteed emotional safety. To leave, we must let go. We say "no" to something in order to say "yes" to something else. We release one thing in order to grasp another. That release may prove wonderful, or it may not. It reminds me of a fortune cookie fortune I have pasted in my journal. Surely it is the best ever: "The near future may bring everything you have always wanted. Then again, it may not."

True. There simply are no guarantees of safety when leavings are elected. Many are the numbers of those who remain in dull, stifling, or even hurtful situations, who close ears and eyes to opportunities, who stymie noble character and reject growth rather than risk a terrifying moment that precedes attachment and follows letting go.

With some structural liberty, I quote Jesus who once said to a questioning young man, "I'll tell you what I want. You let go of your wealth and your reputation and follow me. Just let go."

"Ah," said the financially and morally successful young man, "not even for eternal life can I do that." He was sure and he was safe. He *was* curious. But, he was not willing to leave the familiar.

He was not alone in that human response. "I don't want change." "I need to be sure." "I want to feel safe." "I am powerfully reluctant to be sad and leaving too often produces that opportunity." I recognize those concerns; perhaps you do. I experience them. Some of them sometimes rule my days.

A Reluctance to Be Sad

My decision to attend seminary came loaded with sadness. Granted, not the sadness of tragedy but real sadness, nevertheless. My years of teaching and listening to women stacked to such a rewarding height that those habits seemed impervious to change. School meant capping that stack, leaving what I truly loved doing. Leaving people with whom I loved being and working. Saying "no" to harmful things is hard, but saying "no" to something good in order to say "yes" to another good or something better? Terrible! Dione, a Bible study coworker who knew me well, wrote to me about this in the midst of my vacillations,

> Now to address the question of whether the Lord is moving you out . . . When a person thinks he has an interest in mountain climbing, he begins on a small scale (home Bible studies). [The parenthesis was hers. Dione always makes sure I understand things.]

> There's a rock south of Point Mugu that is a beginner rock for climbers to learn on. It doesn't take much time or investment. If our climber has a natural talent . . . he'll equip himself better—sharpen his skills with experience on more challenging mountains, and get better climbing equipment (study, and $$ in books). If this mountain climber continues to have a unique capability for climbing, then, as circumstances permit, he will invest a great deal of his life in climbing. . . .

By this time he has a lot to offer. Then comes the day he is asked to join an exposition on Mt. Everest. He has been asked because he has established a reputation of being very capable. Will he decline? How can he continue his present work and accept? What painful thinking processes!

. . . By accepting the Mt. Everest exposition, however, he will be weighted with more awesome responsibilities. There will be sacrifices, dangers & failures mixed in with the triumphs. And, definitely a longing for what he has left. But—he's been selected.

She helped me decide to climb a personal Everest. I got lost in tears over goodbyes and well-wishing. I also got lost on the freeway coming home from Pasadena after my day of seminary registration. Freeway #5 will not carry a traveler where #118 will, regardless of good intentions. Magic Mountain's Great Colossus provided a massive clue that I was nowhere near the Oxnard Plain or the Camarillo Ranch. David still shakes his head when I attempt to explain my route home through Valencia, Fillmore, and Grimes Canyon rather than the San Fernando Valley. Actually, the experience was a great metaphor for my feelings of that day. Lost. Separated from this, not yet connected to that. Between things, and sad, and reluctant to be so.

But I made it home, then started school. From the first day, the first hour, the first autumn smell of fertilizer on the campus quad, the first successful return home, I loved it. I managed well. I was sailing along, healing from separations and thriving on the good diet being fed my mind and soul.

Then came spring 1984. With my first year nearly completed, I returned home from a day of class, grabbed the mail from the box on my way down the drive and stepped into our kitchen reading. Suddenly, I slid my back along the refrigerator door, dropping to the floor with a letter in my hand. David stood wondering what my grandmother wrote that hurt me so, that made me so obviously sad. I began reading her letter joyously, as I usually did. Then I came to this:

> I enjoyed your letter so much. Reading about all of the studying you are doing, my heart rejoiced for I could remember all of the times where I would have loved a class room.

> Before I go farther let me say again, "I love you, Darling," but when I got to the part where you had the question, "Why?" [Why am I so fortunate to go to seminary, I had asked.]

> At first I thought, "Of course, we like to learn." Then there came this picture to my mind—a busy little wife and mother—cooking up something for a neighbor who was ill—studying for a large Bible study for women—speaking at Retreats—Mother-Daughter Luncheons—answering the phone and helping someone in a problem—Being close and on an understanding level—You did it, it seemed to me, perfectly. Gave yourself.

> Now, in a higher level, an unlearned one like me would not have the audacity to seek you, you would never understand my problems.

> You took all of this time and labor to satisfy yourself. Do you suppose you could be satisfied to be available for just "down to earth" problems, encouraging someone to try harder to be a better wife, or an understanding mother to a child or teen-ager?

> Wish I could have a good visit with you.

"Dear God," I cried and crumpled to the floor. "How can Granny say this? She is among the dearest of all people to me. Doesn't she know me better than that?" Her letter broke my heart. My gentle Granny, whose death this year saddened me profoundly, preferred my old, familiar habits. They were admirable, safe; she was sure of them. What on earth would I do with an education she felt belonged to men anyway—a graduate degree in theology. Would this make my meals better? Was school distracting me too thoroughly from doing good things for others? Would I get smug? Would it separate us somehow? Many people will resist changes that we make, even people who love us. Or especially people who love us?

Sad? Yes. Well we may be when we make changes. But immobilized when we ought to be moving? Not possible for people who choose to be real. We are reluctant to be sad, but leaving often causes it. It may sound odd to the ear, but the heart needs to hear it: "Be authentically sad." We feel sad when we are affected by grief, sorrow, loss, or unhappiness. Sadness is not anger or blame or denial turned inward. Depression may be, but sadness is not. Often we confuse these reactions. Consequently, our ability to handle any of them properly is also confused. Sadness needs courage, reason, and time, but not correction.

Sadness arises from leaving things, places, situations, but never so profoundly as when we leave people. Or when people leave us. Never is there a greater need for deliberateness than in these cases. I have written about Linda, about our friendship. Now I want to talk about her leaving. My journal will do much of this work. It is still hard, and I am still reluctant to be sad.

Monday, July 2, 1990
  Linda sleeps fitfully and tensely in her private room. [Her]
hyper-sensitivity to sound is that which I recognize as a new

phenomenon since my last visit. What good fortune that I brought along a set of Bach tapes: Saint John Passion, Sonatas, Partitas, concertos. This is, today, her music of choice.

I entered a week of setbacks and warnings of her battle's end. Stronger drugs, aborted attempts at rescuing. Procedures, radiation, hookups, shunts, and valves, all failing. The work Linda and I did together concerned conquering anxiety, meeting and managing pain, arranging pillows, rubbing a swollen body, and maintaining a quiet, darkened room.

Wednesday, July 4th
   "So, do you know what today is?" I asked coming into her room.
   "Yes. It is the day the Lord made. And, it is the Fourth of July."
   "So are you going to rejoice in it?" I asked.
   "I am. I plan to eat some food, take a little walk out of this room, wash my hair."

We did manage a short walk. I managed to stand by as a chest tube was removed and an incision leak was fixed. Oxygen was ordered round the clock; her sluggish blood I learned was shunting. Dilaudid, though increased, was self-administered now and no longer sent her on a drunk. That Wednesday, organized and fastidious Linda needed her routine defined and written down. We deliberately named her routine "No Routine." Her work was to accept the unexpected, to roll with what could not be controlled, to manage what she could—like how much water I should add to properly cover the chipped ice. I never got it right and she let me know.

Saturday, July 7th

What a day this has been. Very difficult for me. Last night I gathered the letters that I have written to Linda since 1965. She has kept them all. So many memories on those pages. Today Lin chooses to talk about her dying. Today is my day to cry, and cry. . . . How can sorrow mix so easily with so much love?

We have two goals: 1) for her to get better enough to go home for a while and 2) to prepare well for death if she cannot rally.

The week of July 1–8 blurs. I spent some nights and every day at the hospital. I pushed pillows under the yet ample buttocks, under swelling legs and feet. I gently rubbed a swollen belly and aching shoulders while Lin and I talked, talked, talked. Of cancer, of what measure of hope, of things to tell people, things to do, her funeral, her personal things; her fears, her hopes, but mostly her very present distress.

By week's end breathing is harder. Oxygen is constant, pain is in her left shoulder. . . . Dark circles lay quietly under Linda's eyes. She speaks with difficulty. Her throat feels constricted. Her body is so swollen. Her eyes roll when they close, . . . she dreams nonsense.

Sunday.

We had a remarkable Sunday afternoon. She was energized for a long period of time . . . two hours? Later I think, maybe she is going to get better.

. . . Marvelous conversation, tears together (she decides to let herself cry). ". . . the medication will keep me from crying too much," she says confidently.

"Barbara, I'm going to take a short little nap. Then, before you leave me today, I want you to bless me. Will you do that?"

I would be leaving her that night, to fly to my home the following morning. Not for the last time, I told myself. In a couple of weeks I would be speaking in Estes Park and before and after my commitment there I planned to spend time with her. Linda, I think, knew better.

> *"I will," I say and I sit, thinking, while she sleeps. Before I leave, with her hands in both of mine, I say through my tears something like this,*
> *"Dearest Linda, I bless you . . . with the gathering up of all our years of love, mingled and preserved for us, forever. May God bless you with a crossing to Eternal Life that bursts with Spring. A gift to you after your hard Winter of suffering.*
> *. . . with my hands, my eyes, my ears, my voice, and thoughts, I bless, you, Linda Houser. I send with you, my heart."*

I lay against her bed quietly crying with her hands in mine. She put her head back on her pillow, smiled, and cried. She said again for the how many hundredth time? "My dear, dear friend, how I love you. . . ." I do not remember that there was an actual goodbye. I rubbed her feet until she slept. I do remember walking out of the hospital into rain. I was so thankful for it. Rain never fails to comfort me. I drove to her home through it and early the next morning left my friend. "For the last time?" asks my journal. Leaving was not in the plan we laid for our friendship.

Leaving life was not what Linda would have chosen for her forty-ninth year. It was a sadness she was reluctant to embrace. But when it became clear that no choices remained, she grabbed it and made leaving a deliberate act. Linda finished life by leaving well.

I could write forever a list of reasons against her absence. But when there was no choice but to be finished with friendship here, we worked to leave it with deliberateness.

Thursday, July 12th

Linda's son, Jon Shannon, called this morning. "Mom has taken a turn for the worse and the doctors say she probably won't make it through the day."

This is the Thursday I bought Shasta daisies and planted them in my yard. This is the day I said for the first time, "Linda has died." The day I wrote,

For once I understand a meaningless moment. She did not die at night, she did not die alone. But she died. Impossible. . . . How long will it take to believe this? I don't need to cry very much, not yet, at least. So much has already been cried through with Linda. Our facing her death has been done quite thoroughly, together, in that hospital. With laughter, tears, fear, and courage. With gifts of words, gifts of tangible things, with tasks done together for the sake of her body and mind. With questions and affirmations for her spirit.

I flew to Denver one more time that July, to "do her service," as Linda said I would. In the eulogy I confessed

that I don't feel like a celebrant. I am admittedly absorbed more in my loss than in her newfound release. I can't "picture" her in Heaven, I'm not completely convinced there are Bing Cherries there [another story, another time]. . . . I'd rather have her here. . . . Even though she and I agreed to prefer the quality of our friendship to a greater number of years, I admit, I am not yet ready to celebrate.

I quoted St. Augustine who wrote in his *Confessions,*

The grief I felt for the loss of my friend had struck . . . into my inmost heart. . . . I wondered that he should die and I remain alive, for I was his second half. Like the poet who called his friend, ". . . the half of his soul!"

How I wish I could report that I "did" that service because I am so wonderful or mature. A lack of such perfection took no more time to appear than it takes an endodontist to finish a root canal. "Doing" that service fulfilled my commitment to Linda and then offered me immediate opportunity to face some work due my character. From my point of view, Linda jumped out of the blocks before the whistle blew, she got a head start on maximizing character, she leapt early to the place where it all began in the beginning. But I stand here, on earth, where imperfection remains and my contribution to it is sometimes powerful, sometimes self-serving, or ugly, or thoughtless. I have plenty of authenticating work to do.

Following Linda's service I moved through conversations of lingering family and friends. "The measure of Barbara Pine got defined," says my journal, when a skinny, dark-eyed woman placed her hands on my shoulders, allowed maudlin tears to spill on her cheeks and through her words. "Oh, thank you for what you said today." Already I resented her tone. "It expressed so perfectly *our* love for *our* Linda."

I wanted to punch her in the nose, says my journal. Anger shot from my gut to my brain shouting inwardly, "I do not share an 'our' Linda. My words expressed MY love, thank you very much." I was hurt, and I was testy at that particular moment. I finally gained enough control to excuse myself, to leave her long-playing, saccharine memories to the ears of others. I did not leave her well.

I am glad, though, to report that Linda and I left friendship deliberately and quite well. We were reluctant to; it made us sad. But sad is a feeling appropriate to many forms of leaving. The good news? Sadness does not require correcting.

Conclusion

I venture to say that when Christopher Columbus left Spain in the 1490s, he left well. Queen Isabella saw to that. I react to his quest for Asia as I do to Voltaire's method of complaining. Both are so wonderfully surprising that I want to hear the accounts again and again. Obviously, I do not tell this story as a historian or for history's sake.

Columbus left. He commanded three ships and ninety men. He planned to sail westward till he reached islands near Japan where he would establish a trading city. Strong winds prevailed, and for ten days the ships battled to stay upright. So they wound up a little "off course." What's a little off, yes? Despite murmuring among the sailors and the absence of land sightings for more than a month, Columbus pressed the voyage forward. Ah, that split second between letting go and grabbing on. Columbus sailed through it and was rewarded! Land ahoy!

Believing he reached Asia, he and his crew explored the Caribbean for ten weeks. Coconuts, cinnamon, a bit of gold, and a few kidnapped "Asians" got loaded aboard the ships for the return trip. The ship's journal called the people hospitable, the ground fertile, the harbors plentiful and marvelous, the rivers flooded with gold. Columbus was right about many things he observed, but he was wrong, really wrong, about one thing—the location. He died believing that he had found the water route to Asia.

What could be worse than being slightly off course? A bit or largely wrong? He could have feared failure and chosen never to leave. If only he could have been "sure of." If only he had waited until he felt safe about it all. Till he knew the true size of the Atlantic. At least until someone told him that the Americas existed, blocking the path to Asia. Or that a great Pacific Ocean lay beyond the Americas and required crossing before any European got to play Pachinko games in Tokyo.

Leavings can occur so naturally, so slowly, that transitions require no more notice than the redistribution of air around us as we walk through a park. Then again, they may be abrupt, jarring, maddening, sorrowful, grievous. Like the hard slap of a branch against our face as we cut through bramble bushes. What we know is that leavings constantly occur. Those who are conscious of them need to be about their tending. That is, any who plan to experience authentic life might plan to be. Follow the example of Columbus; get going. Risk the mistake, the surprise. The rewards.

Ah, the rewards of leaving well. Of leaving a rotten movie and going instead for a good ice cream cone. How good it feels to take a break from writing, leave it, walk on the beach in a gentle rain. Or to move from ironing shirts to plucking weeds. The smell of starch is nice for a while. Leave it. Smell grass, instead. Listen to a blue jay sass his world. The change is restorative. Let bare feet leave hot pavement. Take a deep breath in the midst of a mighty argument, leave it, temporarily, and feel the relief of your own silence. Go out a different door when you leave church. Leave ground turkey or tomato soup off your grocery list; see what changes are required and how refreshing they prove. Slide into slippers after a long day at work; leave the shoes the day wore. Leave the television off; pick up a book or a conversation.

Deliberately leave anger, wrath, and malice, says the apostle Paul. Deliberately commit to mercy, kindness, tolerance, and forgiveness. This, as much as prayer and church attendance, is the work of people who listen to God. Ah, such rhythms of life, of commitment, such singing with grace, as Paul says. Such an admirable dance of noble character.

Leave well, relationships fought for but that must end . . . whether beautifully or tragically. Leave well, that which stubbornly opposes all efforts of tending. Leave well, sloppy attitudes toward your spirit, your body, your mind, your emotions.

Separate, depart, take off, scram. Leave old or new ideas when they prove harmful. Leave the bad for the good. Leave good things for better things. But leave when it is appropriate or required for the development of noble character. Then, leave well. Leave deliberately.

EPILOGUE

"Men travel faster now but I do not know if they go to better things," said Eusibis, a wise old Navajo, in Willa Cather's *Death Comes to the Archbishop*. He noticed that a one-day rail trip completed what took him and his mule two weeks to accomplish. Freeing up time. For what? For better things? For better being?

We moderns, Westerners particularly, move faster and perhaps more freely than any people history has ever known. We have time to do virtually anything and freedom to think as we well please. Along with mule treks and dress shoes we have kicked off nearly every sense of duty to social and moral consensus. Talk about freedom! We can indulge ourselves, deprive ourselves, disavow or espouse any political, religious, educational, moral, or ethical standard; we eschew unified judgment and proudly tolerate everything.

But can it be that in traveling faster and lighter, in having discarded most of the past's culturally-packed baggage, that our liberated personalities are *not* moving to better things? Should we tap our population on the shoulder and point out that we are more neurotic, more violent, more conformed, less creative, less moral, less intellectually curious, more isolated or fragmented, less fulfilled, more anxious, less happy, or less noble than ever before? Is it possible that we tolerate nearly anything because we treasure virtually nothing?

Without a commitment to authentic, noble life, we are passively ruled by the convenient, the contiguous, the comfortable, the quick, the clever, the uncomplicated. Usually the reward of such things is cynicism, weariness, selfishness, a stunted spirit and a defeated ego.

It's tough traveling slowly enough to shape nobility; to stop often enough to linger, listen, learn, lean, loan, laugh, leave; to be real. The Velveteen Rabbit learned this lesson well. From the book with the same title we learn that,

> The Skin Horse had lived longer in the nursery than any of the others. He was so old that his brown coat was bald in patches and showed the seams underneath, and most of the hairs in his tail had been pulled out to string bead necklaces.

The Skin Horse was wise. He knew that manufactured experiences differed greatly from real ones. The Rabbit knew that questions to Skin Horse earned truthful answers. So he asked, "What is REAL? Does it mean having things that buzz inside you and a stick-out handle?"

"Real isn't how you are made," said the Skin Horse. "It's a thing that happens to you. . . ." Who is surprised that Rabbit's next question was, "Does it hurt?" Or that Horse answered, "Sometimes." He added, "When you are Real you don't mind being hurt," but he cautioned against thinking *real* happens instantaneously.

"You become," he counseled. "It takes a long time." It

seldom happens to people who break easily, he said. Seldom to people with "sharp edges," or to those who must be "carefully kept." A noble thought. A long process. A grand experience. Life. With a capital "L."